ADVANCE PRAISE

"Patrick's book explains why every American is experiencing worry, fear, and uncertainty with their finances. Heads I Win, Tails You Lose outlines a better way to take back control and live a life you love."

—MIKE DILLARD, ENTREPRENEUR, AUTHOR, PODCASTER

"This must-read book highlights the importance of knowing your options to manage and grow your wealth, especially in our crazy economy and market."

—KEN MCELROY, CEO OF MC COMPANIES,
RICH DAD ADVISOR, AUTHOR

"Patrick educates the reader in a strategy that creates wealth in a way that is a refreshing alternative to the cookie cutter advice generally given. My family has greatly benefited. It should be seriously considered by any and all looking to develop long-term financial success."

—THOMAS MATTHEW, MD, FACC, FACS; ASSISTANT
PROFESSOR OF SURGERY, DIRECTOR OF JOHNS
HOPKINS CARDIOTHORACIC SURGERY

"Heads I Win, Tails You Lose teaches the novice and the expert how to win, no matter the circumstances."

—MATT SMITH, CEO OF ROYALTY EXCHANGE

"This is one of the few books that has it all. Heads I Win, Tails You Lose shows you the time-tested path to build and protect generational wealth. Plus it gives you the history and hard facts of how blind trust in Wall Street will cost you tens of thousands of dollars."

—JEFF SCHNEIDER, CPA, CIA; COO OF EARLY TO RISE

"A wise read for anyone serious about taking control of their finances outside of the mainstream approach. Heads I Win, Tails You Lose synthesizes the complexities of financial advice into actionable strategies that work."

—JASON HARTMAN, ENTREPRENEUR, REAL ESTATE EXPERT, PODCASTER

"A modern-day primer on the philosophy and spirituality of money, Heads I Win, Tails You Lose borrows from ancient texts, scriptures, and classics to apply wealthy mindsets to today's financial landscape and the opportunities it employs. This is not a book for the kindhearted or 'get rich quick' schemer. It's a deep guide for knowledge-seekers, attainers, polymaths, and artists to be healthy in all facets of life. It's about time a financial planner/advisor shows his passion for

wealth creation through the didactic, written word, and not by uninformed, snake oil sales calls or pitches."

"Patrick is someone that I call upon to learn the strategies of the world's richest people. Heads I Win, Tails You Lose provides a creative approach for managing wealth outside of the old and tired methods used by everyone else."

"Don't be part of the uninformed majority who don't plan well for their future. Read this book and apply Patrick's wisdom and insights to turn the American Dream into your personal reality!"

"This book is a window into Patrick's world of proven and practical wealth strategies that have surprisingly been forgotten. I'd encourage anyone who is fed up with the typical financial planning world and seeking financial freedom to read Heads I Win, Tails You Lose."

"*Heads I Win, Tails You Lose* aligns with my view: conventional financial planning doesn't work. If conventional financial planning worked, our middle class would all become wealthy, right? Patrick would agree with my trademarked quote, 'You can be conventional or you can be wealthy. Pick one.'™ Patrick and I have similar stories in that we crossed paths with the Real Estate Guys and their crowd, and it expanded our paradigms. Patrick is a good friend, and I love hearing his thoughts on economics and finance. This book is a must-read for those who are looking for ways to expand their thinking and wealth outside the conventional ways taught by our mainstream media and others."

—DAVE ZOOK, CEO OF THE REAL ASSET
INVESTOR, OWNER OF HORIZON STRUCTURES

"*Storyteller, man of honor, humble seeker of Truth*—these are the words I think about when Patrick comes to mind. I've been looking forward to this book for quite a while and am pleased to tell you, the reader, it is worth the wait. All human beings go through challenges in their lives—it is what we do with them that makes the difference. Patrick has experienced some (and watched his clients and advisors experience some) on both the financial and health level that caused him to be a good storyteller, an even more honorable man, and a continuous seeker of Truth and Principles. He says I've mentored him, yet he's mentored me just as much. Enjoy his story."

—KIM BUTLER, CEO OF PARTNERS FOR
PROSPERITY, AUTHOR, PODCASTER

"*Financial education is at the heart of investing success during the best of economic times. However, it becomes even more important in the face of economic uncertainty. In seeing this for myself during the last recession and now in working with consumers and small business owners on money and time management, I see just how critical it is that we, as a country, improve our financial literacy. However, Americans generally lack the financial education that they need to make the best decisions in the short and long term. In my own thought leadership, I recommend the value of taking the time to read and learn more to increase financial literacy. And that's exactly what Heads I Win, Tails You Lose: A Financial Strategy to Reignite the American Dream does for readers. It serves as a primer on where to put your money—which is not in a 401(k), bank, or mutual fund. Instead, there are actionable tips related to other sources of real wealth that reminded me I could add more to my financial wisdom bank. The book is chock full of resources to do additional research. Plus, it's easy to read for all levels of financial literacy. It's a must-read for anyone that wants to develop a solid financial foundation and generate more wealth.*"

—JOHN RAMPTON, SERIAL ENTREPRENEUR

"*We are not taught any financial education in schools, colleges, and universities, and as a result, the majority of people find themselves losing in the game of money. As one of the top financial educators, Patrick shares a blueprint of how to take control of your financial life and investments and achieve financial freedom. This book is packed with actionable education, tools, techniques, and powerful financial strategies."*

—M.C. LAUBSCHER, PRESIDENT OF
PRODUCER'S WEALTH, PODCASTER

"In Patrick Donohoe's new book, Heads I Win, Tails You Lose, you will find an easy-to-understand explanation of why our financial system is fractured and how to make sure you are in the driver's seat to achieving financial freedom. Patrick is the real deal."

—KYLE WILSON, FOUNDER OF JIM ROHN
INTERNATIONAL AND AUTHOR OF *52 LESSONS I
LEARNED FROM JIM ROHN AND OTHER LEGENDS*

"Life is all about how you think, as this book teaches. And the way you think about money is one of the most important factors for your health, happiness, and success in life. It determines the strength of your marriage, your children's future, and even the length of your life. That's why Patrick's book is a must-read for anyone seeking wisdom on how to improve their money mindset. If you're tired of being taken for a ride by the financial industry, it's time for you to take back control of your financial future."

—CRAIG BALLANTYNE, OWNER OF EARLY TO RISE
AND AUTHOR OF *THE PERFECT DAY FORMULA*

"I don't have a 401(k) (and I never will). I don't have 529 plans for my kids (won't do that either). I'm stashing my money in the strategies Patrick talks about in Heads I Win, Tails You Lose. When the next mega crash hits, I'll sail right through it unscathed...while the rest stress, panic, and lose their money in the markets. I hope tons of Americans read this book and get with the world-class team Patrick has assembled to get their money safe—before it's too late."

—TIM MITTELSTAEDT, FOUNDER AND
CEO OF DEEPWATER DIGITAL

"Heads I Win, Tails You Lose is an inspiring book that provides a creative approach for managing your wealth outside of the banking system and Wall Street."

—MAURICIO RAULD, FOUNDER OF PREMIER LAW GROUP

"With mainstream financial advice being forced down the throats of the average person, Heads I Win, Tails You Lose is a must-read for anyone who wants real financial strategies."

—JACK AND BRYAN FOUTS, PARTNERS
AT THE ELEVATION GROUP

"You have an epiphany discovering that inflation, emotion, taxes, fees, and volatility often conspire to make real returns from traditional retirement vehicles near zero—a 401(k) is more of a 'Life-Deferral Plan' than a 'Tax-Deferral Plan.'"

—KEITH WEINHOLD, HOST OF THE GET RICH EDUCATION
PODCAST, FORBES CONTRIBUTOR ON REAL ESTATE

HEADS I WIN, TAILS YOU LOSE

HEADS I WIN, TAILS YOU LOSE

A FINANCIAL STRATEGY TO REIGNITE THE AMERICAN DREAM

PATRICK H. DONOHOE

Although the author has made every effort to ensure that the information in this book was correct at press time, the author does not assume and hereby disclaims any liability to any party for any loss, damage, or disruption caused by errors or omissions, whether such errors or omissions result from negligence, accident, or any other cause. This book is also not intended to provide specific financial or legal advice. The author does not assume and hereby disclaims any liability to any party for any loss, damage, or disruption caused by the information in this book. For advice and guidance specific to your situation please contact Paradigm Life, PL Wealth Advisors, or a qualified expert.

HEADS I WIN, TAILS YOU LOSE
A Financial Strategy to Reignite the American Dream

ISBN   978-1-5445-1114-6 *Hardcover*
       978-1-5445-1084-2 *Paperback*
       978-1-5445-1085-9 *Ebook*

LIONCREST
PUBLISHING

I dedicate this book to my three children: Hannah, Meghan, and Jack—I love you more than anything on earth—and to my wife Synthia, the greatest blessing of my life.

CONTENTS

FOREWORD

BY TOM WHEELWRIGHT

Taxes are the biggest bill people pay. The average person's tax bill is up to 50 percent of their income when you add up income, sales, value-added, employment, and the many other forms of tax. When you calculate the time it takes to earn that money, it adds up to years for some and decades for most.

Taxes don't just take your money—they steal your time.

It may not surprise you, but the well-informed individual—typically entrepreneurs, business owners, and investors—pays a fraction of that, and some even pay zero.

This imbalance really upsets people...maybe even you. If it does, I want you to take a deep breath, shake out your body for a moment, sit back down, and try on a new way of thinking. Ask yourself this question:

HOW can you legally pay so little, even zero, in taxes?

In my book, *Tax-Free Wealth*, part of the *Rich Dad Advisor Series*, I answer this question in detail and educate the reader on my views of tax law. The book provides a map to lower your taxes and build massive wealth. Education is the key to navigating this map so you can pay less in taxes and regain years of your life.

Financial education is what fundamentally separates the rich from the poor—the lack of it is why most people pay so much in taxes, why many fall short of building wealth, and why few ever achieve financial freedom. Having spent over 35 years in the financial sector, specifically in taxes, I am a firsthand witness of the importance of education.

I started at a 'Big Four' accounting firm, worked for a Fortune 1000 company, moved to an international accounting firm, and then formed my own practice that specializes in tax and wealth strategies for business owners and investors. On top of that, I get to travel the world as a Rich Dad Advisor, speaking alongside my mentor, friend, and client Robert Kiyosaki. Together we teach audiences in dozens of different countries about money, mindset, and financial freedom.

My experience makes me confident that anyone who wants to live a more abundant life can—including you. But you must first understand that it comes with a price tag: education.

Taking the time to inform yourself and focus your efforts can make your dreams a reality. Whatever motivated you to pick up this book is a sign that you want this for yourself, so congratulations on taking the first step in seeking out someone who can teach you.

Once in a great while, a person comes along who can explain financial concepts so clearly that all of a sudden, what had been a mystery becomes obvious. For many people, Robert Kiyosaki was that person when he wrote **Rich Dad Poor Dad**. For me, that person was Patrick Donohoe when he first explained what you're about to learn in this book.

Patrick draws on a lifetime of experience to explain the importance of a healthy financial philosophy, mindset, and the ins and outs of strategies that are outside of the mainstream understanding.

As an author myself, I have genuine respect for all that it takes to develop and produce a book that has value and truly serves its audience. Patrick's *Heads I Win, Tails You Lose: A Financial Strategy to Reignite the American Dream* does that exceptionally well.

Many years ago, my good friend, Kim Butler, introduced me to Patrick. Since I was from Salt Lake City and Patrick lives in Salt Lake City, she thought we might share some common interests.

Patrick sat down with me to explain how to leverage a mutual insurance company as part of one's personal wealth strategy—similar to how banks, corporations, and wealthy people use them. It wasn't until then that I realized how beneficial his specialty was to an investment portfolio.

I remember clearly the conversation when Patrick explained that most people use insurance companies to protect themselves from losses like death, disability, and illness—events that are statistically not likely to happen while you are insured. He continued to teach me that there is another way to use them with a guaranteed outcome.

Banks, big corporations, and notable individuals figured out how to use these types of companies to help them grow their liquid assets tax-free and still have access to their money for other uses like investments or purchases.

As soon as Patrick started talking about taxes, I was hooked. I have since learned, after many conversations with him and through research of my own, the various ways to use what he teaches as part of a comprehensive strategy to build wealth and achieve financial freedom.

The other thing I really like about Patrick is he is an educator of the many aspects of wealth building—investing, tax strategy, business strategy, estate planning, and entrepreneurship; he's not a one-trick pony.

If you want to understand how to make your financial dreams a reality, you are in the right place. Patrick is able to explain how to incorporate his strategy and product expertise in clear, understandable language, so even a hardheaded accountant like me who knows the numbers can understand.

Since our first introduction, Patrick and I have become good friends. We have worked together on many educational projects, cruised around the Caribbean with our wives learning about real estate, and have been partners in several ventures. In every case, Patrick has been a terrific partner and loyal friend. He is a terrific example for young entrepreneurs to emulate. His ethics are outstanding, and he is always fair and generous with both his time and his money.

Patrick tells me that he looks up to me. What he doesn't realize is how much I look up to him. If you want to learn from a great entrepreneur, terrific teacher, and amazing person, I encourage you to pay close attention to what Patrick Donohoe has to say.

TOM WHEELWRIGHT, CPA

AUTHOR AND ENTREPRENEUR

INTRODUCTION

Americans are losing the game of money! *Heads I Win, Tails You Lose* teaches you how to win. You will learn to strategically stack the odds in your favor and ultimately achieve financial freedom, regardless of your present circumstances. You can end up on top, no matter what, and live the American Dream.

> *"Freedom is the open window through which pours the sunlight of the human spirit and human dignity."*
>
> —HERBERT HOOVER

Freedom is our innate human tendency, yet that beacon of Americanism has dimmed over the last 100 years. It's an abstraction to some and a fantasy to others.

Our society has replaced the foundational principles of liberty, self-reliance, entrepreneurship, charity, and unity with safety, security, dependency, mediocrity, self-aggrandizement, and entitlement.

The onus of our collective well-being has been placed on the shoulders of government to create our jobs, balance the economy, give liquidity to financial markets, provide healthcare, clean up the environment, and much more. This was never the intention of our great country. In fact, these are the very reasons that motivated our country's formation in the first place.

The price we have paid for this transference of responsibility continues to compound, as evidenced by these incomprehensible statistics:

THE PRICE

Poor fiscal and monetary stewardship:

- The US National Debt is at an all-time high—over $20 trillion.[1]
- Half of our earned income goes to taxes when you factor in sales and property taxes, utilities, and inflation.[2]
- Social Security and Medicare promises are 200 percent of GDP.[3]

---

1   www.usdebtclock.org

2   https://www.nerdwallet.com/blog/taxes/how-much-do-americans-really-pay-taxes-2015/

3   https://www.ssa.gov/oact/trsum/

Americans lack financial education:

- The retirement savings gap is at $14 trillion.[4]
- Consumer debt is at an all-time high—over $20 trillion.[5]
- Forty-five percent of the workforce has $3,000 saved for retirement.[6]
- Less than 20 percent of the US workforce is highly confident they will be able to retire.[7]

The education system has failed:

- Education expenses keep rising, with marginal (if any) improvement in results.[8]
- Outstanding student loan debt is over $1.5 trillion.[9]
- The student loan default rate is over 50 percent.[10]
- Employment satisfaction and engagement are staggeringly low.[11]
- We have double-digit underemployment.[12]

---

4   https://www.nirsonline.org/reports/the-retirement-savings-crisis-is-it-worse-than-we-think/

5   www.usdebtclock.org

6   https://www.nirsonline.org/reports/the-retirement-savings-crisis-is-it-worse-than-we-think/

7   https://www.ebri.org/pdf/surveys/rcs/2017/IB.431.Mar17.RCS17..21Mar17.pdf

8   https://www.cato.org/blog/public-school-spending-theres-chart

9   https://fred.stlouisfed.org/series/SLOAS

10   https://www.brookings.edu/research/
     the-looming-student-loan-default-crisis-is-worse-than-we-thought/

11   https://cdn.imperative.com/media/public/Global_Purpose_Index_2016.pdf

12   https://www.statista.com/statistics/205240/us-underemployment-rate/

A FLICKER OF LIGHT

"It is during our darkest moments that we must focus to see the light."

—ARISTOTLE

There is hope!

For over 200 years, the torch of liberty has been carried by individuals, businesses, and organizations during such difficult times. They have cleared the path with advancements in every aspect of life. Entrepreneurs have proven what the individual can create by recognizing the true nature of the American Dream. The results are a miraculous testament of what humankind can accomplish when the proper internal and external environments exist to foster such growth.

Dim as it might seem, the embers of the Dream continue to burn. Despite the sobering statistics above, there exists today the sparks of ingenuity from those who are rebelling against the status quo, regaining control of their lives, solving the world's problems, capitalizing on financial and employment opportunities, and becoming wealthy and free in the process. They have reignited the spirit of the American Dream.

The opportunity today to achieve a life of fulfillment, which includes financial freedom, is available to more people than ever before—including you. This achievement is the quintessence of life and is absolutely possible for you. It may come in different forms; however, there are a few key components that are universal:

1. Taking control of your wealth
2. Establishing passive income or cash flow investments
3. Discovering a profession based on purpose, not necessity

The ideal environment to accomplish these ends exists today. Now it's time to stake your claim.

AN INVITATION FOR YOU

"Education is the key to unlock the golden door of freedom."

—GEORGE WASHINGTON CARVER

This book will teach you many of the principles and strategies to help discover your own path to financial freedom. Most importantly, it will show you the mindset required to carry out a successful plan.

A change in mindset, often referred to as a paradigm shift, may require you to question everything you *think* you know about lifestyle, professional career, money management, investing, retirement, and wealth.

The conventional paradigm or mindset that pervades through American society begins in the educational system, is reinforced by the workplace, and is codified by the massive financial services sector. The by-product of this conventional way of thinking is measurable, and the results are clear that it's not working.

From a financial perspective, almost everything you will gain from this book conflicts with what the typical financial planner, financial celebrity, and most financial publications tell you to do. To achieve different results, your mindset, and subsequently your strategy, must change.

"The definition of insanity is doing the same thing over and over again and expecting a different result."

—ALBERT EINSTEIN

Together, we will explore the most common retirement and financial planning topics, such as the 401(k), the stock market, debt, the notion of retirement at 65, and more. We will uncover the actual results and outcomes from history and compare them to widely believed assumptions.

You will then discover how to pivot the foundation of your wealth to one of the safest and most secure financial institutions, the private mutual insurance company. These institutions replace many of the roles that Wall Street and banks are currently playing today. You will learn how to store your wealth with them using a uniquely designed life insurance policy. You will ascertain ways to use this financial tool to make more money in your personal life, business, other investments, and assets you may have already acquired.

You will not be alone on the journey. I will guide you using my story and the stories of several of my clients, many of whom may have been in similar circumstances to yours. Their pursuit of financial freedom led them to take control of their financial life by educating themselves and implementing sound financial strategies.

You sit in a similar seat to Neo in the blockbuster movie *The Matrix*. The outstretched hands of Morpheus are in front of you, offering a choice:

"You take the blue pill, the story ends. You wake up in your bed and believe whatever you want to believe. You take the red pill, you stay in Wonderland, and I show you how deep the rabbit hole goes."[13]

Now, through a new paradigm, let's make it happen!

RESOURCES FOR THIS BOOK

What I have to share stretches far beyond what could fit in

---

13   *The Matrix*, directed by The Wachowski Brothers, Warner Brothers Pictures, 1999.

k. Therefore, I decided to create a digital compan-
) the book, *The Financial Strategy Study Guide*, that you can access for free at headsortailsiwin.com/Study-Guide. This guide will expand on the various ideas covered within these pages and help further your education with applicable media, resources, and references. You have complimentary access to it, so go check it out.

All calculations were made using the Truth Concepts™ software.[14]

---

14   www.truthconcepts.com

CHAPTER 1

ORIGINS OF THE AMERICAN DREAM

"The American Dream is independence and being able to create that dream for yourself."

—MARSHA BLACKBURN

Allow me to rewind the clock a few hundred years to the origins of what has become my financial philosophy—what I consider the American Dream.

One individual epitomized the pursuit of the foundational American ideals and coined a phrase that still echoes today. It is rightfully the backbone of this book and a motivation for you to realize the opportunities ahead.

> *"That being all equal and independent, no one ought to harm another in his **Life**, **Health**, **Liberty**, or **Property**."*
>
> —JOHN LOCKE

The iconic phrase, or rather sequence of words, was conceived in late 17th-century England amid a period of widespread social revolution. Some consider the events that unfolded one of the epicenters of revolutionary thought that eventually led to the American Revolution and, subsequently, the greatest period of human ingenuity, industry, and prosperity up to that point in history.

In 1689, English philosopher John Locke published his *Second Treatise of Government*. In it, he claimed that no man or government has any right or claim on another's life, liberty, and property. The inspiration behind the phrase is as old as time, yet so simple. The philosophy traces back to Socrates, Plato, Aristotle, the Stoics, and the Epicureans. Such rights were the bridge to what the Greeks called *eudaimonia* (ultimate fulfillment), which is evident in Thomas Jefferson's replacement of the word *property* with *happiness* in the Declaration of Independence.

Locke and others fought courageously for ideals that they would never end up experiencing. They hoped that the *inalienable* rights they trumpeted would be protected in the framework of future society. Locke was convinced that the inevitable result would be prosperity.

FINANCIAL FREEDOM AND PROSPERITY

Today, the result of Locke's dream occurs daily, but very few recognize the link between the rights of life, liberty, and property, and humanity's undeniable prosperity.

We're not reading and writing by candlelight, traveling on horseback, being warmed solely by a fireplace, fending off life-threatening diseases, or questioning where our food will come from tonight.

The advances of our world are all traced to these three simple words. They create the ideal environment for human genius to be exercised to conquer the inefficiencies of the world.

This book is a focused education on how to incorporate these fundamental principles into your finances and your life. The teachings are an aggregation of experience that I have been fortunate to gain over the course of more than a decade in business, working with people in every walk of life.

You will learn the details of unique financial strategies and tools that embrace these fundamental principles. They will result in personal financial freedom and the opportunity to make the greatest impact on your family, your business, your community, and your nation.

LIFE: YOU ARE YOUR GREATEST ASSET

"If money is your hope for independence, you will never have it. The only real security that a man will have in this world is a reserve of knowledge, experience, and ability."

—HENRY FORD

Our life is the foundation of wealth, and all other rights and principles are corollaries to it. Our life belongs to us, and likewise, the life of another is theirs and cannot be claimed by us. Life is the context in which we experience everything, and without it, nothing else would matter.

When the environment of life is free, the dynamic sets in motion an innate ingenuity to nurture, improve, and subsequently optimize our physical world. This same motivation carries directly to the same stewardship over our most precious and valuable asset—ourselves.

The result?

Our personal drive to grow and progress will grow stronger. The desire to discover how to be the most valuable to others will intensify. The exchange for that value is not only material wealth but the remuneration of fulfillment and freedom.

Unlike other assets that are finite in nature, there is no end to your degree of understanding, knowledge, education, training, and capacity to be the greatest value to the greatest number of people.

Your capacity to build wealth is unlimited.

Investment in you takes precedence.

Each of us has a unique genius inside waiting to express itself for the benefit of others; it is an asset waiting to be discovered, enhanced, and made even more valuable.

LIBERTY: THE GOAL OF FINANCIAL STRATEGY

"They who can give up essential Liberty to obtain a little temporary Safety, deserve neither Liberty nor Safety."

—BENJAMIN FRANKLIN

For well over a hundred years, the meaning of liberty has arguably decayed as we have delegated more and more responsibility to third parties to care for our well-being, such as government, investment firms on Wall Street, and banks.

The financial education of society today is starting to fit snugly into that popular quote by Benjamin Franklin.

The typical American narrative of going to school, getting a college education, establishing a high-paying job, funding a 401(k), and retiring at 65 is not freedom, and it is diametrically opposed to the American Dream.

The slow and steady permeation of these ideas began in the educational system, made its way to the factory-style work environment, then to the promises of retirement, and finally to the bequeathing of wealth into the hands of Wall Street and the financial services industry.

Today, the more funding pre-college education receives, the worse the outcome is.[15] Despite record profits for universities, there is record student loan debt. Entry-level wages remain stagnant, and underemployment is in the double-digit range.[16]

---

15 https://www.forbes.com/sites/prestoncooper2/2017/07/13/
    new-york-fed-highlights-underemployment-among-college-graduates/#11bbc61240d8

16 http://time.com/money/4658059/college-grads-workers-overqualified-jobs/; https://www.
    statista.com/statistics/205240/us-underemployment-rate/

The broken education system and the mindset of factoryism has bled into the modern workplace, where careers are the function of making money by following orders and where hierarchical management is the law.

The carrot of a future retirement comes from the desire for liberty. It has become an elusive reward, and for most, it's just enough motivation to repeat the cumbersome daily grind.

Many are convinced that the American Dream is retirement, which means "to be taken out of service." The concept of retirement with a state-paid pension comes from Otto von Bismarck, the statesman who was the first Chancellor of the German Empire between 1871 and 1890. Bismarck is remembered for statements like, "Politics is the art of the possible," and, "Laws are like sausages; it is better not to see them being made." He's also the architect of the modern social welfare state, including old age pensions. In Bismarck's day, few people lived to the age of 70, when old age pensions started. Life expectancy in the 1880s was less than 60 years. Today, retirement age is generally 65, and average life expectancy in the US is 81 years for a woman and 76 years for a man. In Bismarck's time, someone who was 70 was considered very old and was probably not capable of working. In our own time, most people at 70 are still physically and mentally active. The equivalent retirement age of today would be 93.

The notion of retirement today is not grounded in the principles of liberty and freedom. There exists a dependence on third parties like Wall Street, banks, and the government for our financial welfare. Wall Street must look out for our best interests and subsequently perform and make money. The US government must be fiscally responsible and avoid wasteful spending above and beyond their means. This expectation is, unfortunately, not the world we live in, and it's a risky proposition to assume it will change.

The dynamic of financial freedom is accomplished in two ways. First, by taking back control of your wealth, which requires eliminating the dependence on third parties and educating yourself to invest in what you understand. Second, it is by investing in yourself to make more money because you are more valuable to others, which initiates the discovery of employment or business that aligns with your genius, passion, and calling.

"If you do what you love, you'll never work a day in your life."

—MARC ANTHONY

PROPERTY: THE ROLE OF RESOURCES

The pursuit of property isn't buying a condo or investment real estate. It's the magical outcome of combining the resources outside of us with those resources inside of us.

When the intention aligns with true capitalism, service, and value provided to another, wealth happens.

Fortunately, we live in a country that allows for such pursuit without much restraint. The environment is ripe and full of opportunities for all.

The physical world we experience has always had the potential to be what it is today. The material to make a computer, a television, a car, or an airplane has always been here. When humankind was free to pursue it without the fear of recourse, their minds began solving the matters that kept humankind in the dark for millennia.

Today, the average American lives better than kings of old.

Humanity has solved inefficiencies in health, food, shelter, clothing, transportation, communication, and entertainment by combining the internal resources with those resources externally.

What you bring to the world is unique and infinite in scope. The world is full of challenges awaiting your mind to come up with solutions.

"I've learned that fear limits you and your vision. It serves as blinders to what may be just a few steps down the road for you. The journey is valuable, but believing in your talents, your abilities, and your self-worth can empower you to walk down an even brighter path. Transforming fear into freedom—how great is that?"

—SOLEDAD O'BRIEN

KEY TAKEAWAYS

- Humankind instinctively seeks growth, and the ideal environment for growth is freedom. No matter how much we try, we can't stand still: "Our human nature compels all of us to move and change throughout our lives. At the same time, nobody who thinks about life wants to experience it as a vegetable. We want to improve and continue to develop mentally."[17]
- You will always be your greatest asset. Invest in yourself first to be more valuable to others. That is true wealth.
- Everyone has a unique genius they bring to the world and has a stewardship to share it.
- Control over your financial life equals freedom.

---

17   *The Master Key System*, by Charles Haanel.

CHAPTER 2

THE PERPETUAL WEALTH STRATEGY™

The Perpetual Wealth Strategy is the creation and expertise of my firm, Paradigm Life. It has transformed the lives of thousands of our clients.

The strategy is the utilization of financial vehicles offered by a private mutual insurance company. These financial vehicles provide you with the means to regain control of your finances and build wealth outside of Wall Street.

Who it works for:

- For the executive employee, it replaces your 401(k) or can complement it by providing no annual limits on what you can contribute.

- For families with children, it provides superior growth, liquidity, and control over the typical 529 plan.
- For real estate investors, the strategy can give you a superior yield on your liquid savings and enhance the performance of your property portfolio.
- For business owners, it offers unmatchable privacy and asset protection, while still giving you control based on its liquidity. You will learn about a way to offer it as an incentive to your executives using IRC 162 instead of a 401(k) or profit-sharing plan.
- For those 50 years and older and planning on "retirement" within 15 years, it accelerates that time frame to as little as five years by positioning assets to generate guaranteed cash flow, maximize Social Security benefits, and minimize income tax, all within the same strategy.

My story is congruent to an economic idea by Austrian Economist Joseph Schumpeter called "creative destruction." Creative destruction identifies the nature and purpose of failure. Adversity engages the process of learning, discovery, and ultimately, *creation* to prevent future failure. The Perpetual Wealth Strategy was conceived during a time of personal and widespread economic failure.

> *"Just as nature takes every obstacle, every impediment, and works around it—turns it to its purposes, incorporates it into itself—so, too, a rational being can turn each setback into raw material and use it to achieve its goal."*
>
> —MARCUS AURELIUS

Here is how it all happened.

THE STORY

September 2008 to October 2009 was one of the darkest times of my adult life. It was a daily battle to drag myself out of bed, only to face the near-impossible war of keeping my business alive. I was overweight. My energy came from Red Bull, and the quality of my food didn't really matter. I owed millions and was responsible for tens of thousands of dollars in monthly payments. I barely saw my wife and kids; I sometimes went days without even talking with them. Every month started with questioning whether I could survive one more month.

LEADING UP TO THE *GREAT RECESSION*

My business went from success to the brink of failure within a matter of months. It was like a tidal wave. Paradigm Life, which was formed toward the end of 2007 in partnership with two other financial service companies, had a successful start. I operated Paradigm, and my partners ran their respective operations that were tied to mortgage and real estate investment. Then the Great Recession of 2008 hit.

The businesses within the partnership began to unravel as real estate prices dropped and demand for mortgage lending disappeared. The business environment was completely different. Nobody wanted to invest or was even willing to learn about anything that had to do with finance. People were losing their jobs and homes; they were cashing out of their retirement accounts—even after those accounts lost more than half their value. One by one, the partners left, and we disbanded the entire organization in the summer of 2009.

I was running out of money quickly, and my energy and drive weren't far behind. My advisors, friends, and family told me to just hang it up, file bankruptcy, and start over. I spent a lot of time on my knees and many hours pacing the empty offices, searching for guidance and inspiration to know what to do.

What was left of my rational thinking kept leading me to one plan: file for bankruptcy, unload the various rental properties and other assets, sell everything we could from the office and house, and move to Phoenix to be closer to my wife's family. We would make a fresh new start. We found a place to live, had the moving van arranged, and were within weeks of leaving. Little did I know, however, that a few miracles were brewing.

Through my personal experience and those of others, I have learned over the years that in the depths of despair, serendipity works its magic.

AN APPRENTICESHIP BEGINS

In the months leading up to the climactic panic of the financial crisis, I had hosted dozens of webinars and met with at least 200 people, yet I only did business with 28. The nature of the presentations and meetings was to teach them how to structure a specific type of life insurance that diversified their savings and retirement assets away from Wall Street and banks. The financial vehicles I was able to offer them had a contractually guaranteed rate of growth and the potential to earn a dividend, both tax-free. On top of that, the insurance company offered policyowners a line of credit secured by the policy itself, which was an ideal alternative to traditional bank loans.

Working against me was the feeling of euphoria that was still lingering, as stock market and real estate prices were within a few percentage points of all-time highs. The growth and gains people were experiencing made the idea of diversifying to more secure assets pointless.

Then the crisis hit. In October, the DOW hit a low of 7,062—it had been 5,700 points higher six months before. In that same period of time, the unemployment rate doubled to 7.2 percent, and over 11 million people were out of work. More than 800,000 people lost their homes, and more than 3.1 million people were issued foreclosure notices.

It was a blood bath.

REBIRTH

After more than a year of turmoil, the autumn of 2009 was when I almost gave up. Ironically, that was when several glimmers of hope appeared. The first was a voicemail out of the blue from a local real estate investment company. The owners had heard about Paradigm Life from one of my former colleagues and were intrigued by our unique financial strategies. After a brief return phone call, we agreed there might be a possible business relationship.

The second sign of light at the end of the tunnel was a business conference I had been invited to because of Paradigm's success during the first half of 2008. The meetings were to take place in Europe, all-expenses paid. Last, business started to pick up a bit as the entire country had lost faith in the typical market investments and were seeking stability.

So, with a few glimmers of hope on the horizon and the

business on its last shoestring, Synthia and I boarded a plane to Prague with barely $150 to spend. We didn't know then that this trip would not only save our marriage, but save the business, too. From Prague, we went to Germany and boarded a riverboat that would, over the next five days, carry us down the Danube River with a group of other financial professionals.

MEETING MENTORS

One of the attendees of the conference was Nelson Nash, author of *Becoming Your Own Banker* and *Building Your Warehouse of Wealth*. On this trip, Nelson, with 83 years of experience under his belt, became one of my mentors. I consider the conversation we had on the first afternoon of the cruise the most pivotal dialogue of my life.

I was exploring the ship with a newfound friend when we saw Nelson and his wife on the opposite side of the top deck. As we strolled over, it began to drizzle. I distinctly remember his southern Alabama accent and what he said: "Life is all about how you think, man. The world is upside down because, today, nobody knows how to think for themselves—they just follow. That's why they all lost their homes and their money." Nelson knew that the financial crisis at hand would happen; he had seen it before. He went on to challenge me to read and study the works that taught and inspired him. Books on economics, losophy, and financial strategy, such as *The Law* by ?deric Bastiat, *Economics in One Lesson* by Henry Hazlitt, *The Mainspring of Human Progress* by Henry Weaver, and *How Capitalism Saved America* by Thomas DiLorenzo. Nelson changed my life that day.

Also aboard was Kim Butler and her husband Todd Langford. Kim is the author of several books, including *Busting the Retirement Lies, Busting the Financial Planning Lies, Busting the Interest Rate Lies,* and *Live Your Life Insurance.* She was one of the first advisors to Robert Kiyosaki, most famous for his bestselling book *Rich Dad Poor Dad.* Kim is the founder of the Prosperity Economics Movement, a nonprofit organization that mentors financial advisors and teaches them to base their advice on principle, not product. She's also a business coach for the highly regarded company, Strategic Coach, in Toronto and Chicago. I had known Kim since 2005. She was one of the main inspirations for the formation of Paradigm Life.

Assuming Kim was experiencing similar effects from the Great Recession, I was anxious for her counsel on the direction she was taking and where I should be going. As intuitive and insightful as she had been for years, her advice to me wasn't much different. She remained certain that the financial principles we mutually subscribed to and the surety of the financial strategies we both taught would shine through this dark financial period.

However, there was a twist. Kim's husband Todd had just that year developed a software program called Truth Concepts, a tool that illustrated *all* financial strategies objectively and ultimately reinforced ours with empirical precision. Their excitement about it was contagious, and they were adamant that I attend a training that following year. The Truth Concepts software ended up being foundational to my future and the future of Paradigm Life.

When I arrived home, I felt like a new person: more committed to my wife and family than ever, and more committed to my business. I was determined to dig myself out, no matter how hard it would be or how long it would take.

We endured some challenging days from 2009 to 2011, as did the whole US economy, but we were able to hang on and not shut the doors. The education I gained about banking, creditor and consumer laws, bankruptcy law, the collection industry and subsequent laws, and foreclosure and real estate law, gave me a perspective on the financial industry that can only be described as loathing, and it fueled my passion even more. It gave me the ammunition to help clients and prospective clients navigate the challenging financial waters and ensure their financial life was bulletproof going forward.

I had thousands of conversations and hosted hundreds of webinars. I saw firsthand the effects of the financial calamity. Portfolio and investment loss, excessive debt, unemployment, bankruptcy, and foreclosure. I heard about divorce, abuse, suicide, and homelessness. It was heart-wrenching, but only strengthened my resolve to make a difference with what I knew.

The financial strategies I teach also provided myself and my company the resources necessary to weather the storm. I established my own insurance policies before the financial crisis that were instrumental in helping me make it through—they provided asset protection and credit during a time when I needed it most. My credit scores were ruined because the business debt I personally guaranteed had defaulted. The typical bank account is susceptible to garnishment, which means that if a creditor takes you to court and files a judgment against you, they could give that document to a bank and the bank would freeze your account and give them the money. (You can visit headsortailsiwin.com/StudyGuide to watch my video about some of the horror stories with creditors.)

le to store cash in my policies without the fear

of garnishment because, in the state of Utah, they are protected from this type of garnishment. The line of credit the insurance company provides is guaranteed, and I was able to use it for many years to fund overhead expenses, marketing campaigns, and then used it to pay all my creditors.

PEOPLE AND RELATIONSHIPS ARE LIFE'S GREATEST ASSETS

The myriad of distinct topics of conversation seemed like they were perfectly designed for me. The experience of those on board spanned well past the crisis we were in. They had seen similar economies of the early 2000s, late 1990s, and even earlier. Looking back, with every conversation there seemed to be a growing light at the end of the tunnel. Their willingness to mentor, encourage, and share their war stories was the fuel I had been lacking those last few months before. That trip—lasting just a few short days—resurrected something inside me that had died. I promised Synthia and myself that we would make it through.

I returned from this life-changing 10-day voyage with a renewed mindset and a contagious optimism for the future.

The real estate investment group that expressed interest in a joint venture partnership before the trip came to fruition. It was perfect timing. I was able to retain Dan, who is currently the COO of Paradigm, and Whitney, the Chief of Staff—my two loyal team members—while we got back on our feet. I decided not to file bankruptcy and was adamant about being whole with my creditors.

Over the ensuing months, I had jam-packed 12-hour days and was fueled by a fire that had been on the brink of being extinguished. I gained invaluable experience with the real estate investment group. I learned how to implement our unique financial strategies to enhance the opportunity of buying real estate in one of the best markets in decades.

The success allowed the team (four, including me at the time) to move offices. The lingering memories of pre-2008 were still floating around at the old office. The physical move helped to officially close that chapter of my personal and professional life.

THE REAL ESTATE GUYS

"These emails and calls won't stop coming in," exclaimed Dan, currently COO of Paradigm.

"What did you do?" I responded.

"It's that ad we did with The Real Estate Guys. It's working!" He responded with the excitement of a kid whose chemistry set experiment actually worked.

Soon after the office move, I rekindled a relationship from the pre-2008 era with *The Real Estate Guys* (TREG). TREG was a radio show out of San Jose, California, and at the time, in 2010, the most popular real estate investing podcast. (It's still ranked as one of the top investing podcasts on iTunes today, with over 500 episodes.) Given TREG's affinity toward Robert Kiyosaki and the Rich Dad Poor Dad philosophy, I decided to team up with Kim Butler, who was closely associated with Kiyosaki's work. Together we provided education to their audience about financial principles and strategies that would enhance the financial results for a real estate investor. I didn't anticipate the degree of response from their audience. The market correction and corresponding foreclosures of 2008 and 2009 presented a tremendous opportunity for real estate investors to buy investment properties at a fraction of their market value. The momentum not only boosted listenership profoundly, but it also increased interest in ways to manage wealth outside of the system that just collapsed.

The Real Estate Guys had challenges of their own during the Great Recession and, as a result, were more liberal to the paid sponsors. They began getting a lot of inquiries from their audience regarding our ad, e-book, and strategic recommendations, which included real estate investment. Russell Gray, the co-host of the podcast, reached out and invited Dan and me to San Jose to do an interview to get to know us. (Later, we would learn that the real reason was to make sure we were a legitimate business.) You can listen to that episode from 2011 on their website.[18] I sound so young!

When we arrived in San Jose, we met up for lunch and each member of the Real Estate Guys was there: Robert Helms, Russel Gray, and Bob Helms. We quickly realized how common our financial philosophies were. They had never heard of the strategies we use. They couldn't believe it worked, especially when most investors were finding it nearly impossible to get credit the traditional way.

We also shared a mutual passion. They too were on a crusade to figure out how the economic tidal wave had caught everyone off guard. They wanted to know who the individuals were who foresaw the crash and how they knew. We immediately dove into economics, mainly discussing the Austrian School theory of the business cycle. Two years earlier, I had taken Nelson Nash's challenge to heart and had been obsessed with how those who knew the crisis was coming had figured it out. Most of the books Nelson recommended were from free-market economists, most of whom aligned with what is known today as the Austrian School of Economics. The theory, developed by

18   http://realestateguysradio.libsyn.com/what_is_your_risk_paradigm_a_life_or_debt_decision

Ludwig von Mises, Nobelist Friedrich Hayek, and (claimed that the boom and bust nature of the bus cycle was the inevitable result of stimulus originating from a central bank monetary policy. The conversation was music to my ears.

SUMMIT AT SEA

A few months later, they invited me to be a faculty member on their annual Summit at Sea, a real estate investor conference that takes place on a seven-day cruise. Although Synthia and I had planned our first getaway in over five years that very same week, I agreed to do it. In my ignorance, I assured her that I only had to speak on one of the days and that we would enjoy the cruise ship and ports of call the remainder of the time. Boy, was I wrong.

We arrived in beautiful Fort Lauderdale late the evening before the event started. The next day, we made our way to the kickoff event, where they introduced the speakers and covered the week's itinerary. I have never seen Synthia's eyes so wide. She was livid and would have let me have it had it not been for the hundred others in the room. She was very skeptical about real estate investing, given the hardships we experienced with many of our properties that were acquired toward the end of 2007. She managed the few we had left. Needless to say, real estate was a sore spot for her.

The entire week consisted of education, breakout sessions, cocktail parties, and dinner together. Additionally, each port day involved other activities with the group—no room for vacation. It took Synthia about a day, but she got over it, and by the end of the cruise, she was enthusiastic about getting back into real estate investing.

As a faculty member, I sat on panels, hosted a dinner table each night, and gave an individual presentation for 45 minutes. Although I had done hundreds of webinars and thousands of individual meetings, both live and via web, a live presentation in front of a group was not my forte at all. I was very nervous, and a member of the crowd capitalized on the opportunity.

My presentation consisted of talking about the financial crisis, why the real estate market collapsed, economics, and how the country is taught to trust that banks and Wall Street have our best interests in mind. I then started tying in how to take back control and educate yourself on investments with cash flow. I started explaining how to use a mutual insurance company to store your liquidity, use their guaranteed line of credit to pay off high-interest debt, and buy assets with that cash flow.

Before I could bring the threads of the presentation together, an interruption from the crowd disrupted my flow. A voice called out, "So, I have a question. How do you get paid?" My heart sank—the question completely derailed me. The inquisitor was an older faculty member. He already had an established rapport with the entire group, including The Real Estate Guys. I tried to answer coherently, but it came out sounding very awkward. I said something like, "Well, I don't get paid anything until someone sees the value in what I do and then we're paid by the financial companies we represent." His eye-rolling reaction was all that was needed to keep the frog in my throat. Then, as I tried to continue, he said, "I don't know about you guys, but for the last 10 minutes I have sat here not understanding anything Patrick just said." And then it happened. He turned to Russ and Robert, The Real Estate Guys, and rhetorically asked, "Are you guys following this?"

I was sweating bullets, and Synthia was too. Then, a knight in shining armor came to the rescue. In the crowd was a client I had done business with about a year earlier. He spoke up and stated that he spent months meeting with me and learning about what we did and alluded to it being one of the best financial decisions he had made in a long time. He used his insurance policy as liquidity for his business instead of a bank account and then used the line of credit to purchase construction equipment and fund operational expenses. Additionally, he bought rental property, using the lending provision. Fortunately, others who I had done business with were on the cruise. Over the next few days, they would reinforce the points laid out in my presentation and how they were using the strategy.

Every year since, I have attended The Real Estate Guys Investor Summit at Sea as a faculty member alongside many other iconic names in the financial world.

In 2011, a lot of prayers would be answered. We were swamped with business, and I needed help desperately. Not uncommonly, many clients of Paradigm end up being evangelists of the strategy, to the point where the shifting economy caused a few of them to look deeply into their careers and futures. The next several advisors to join the Paradigm team were clients who ended up leaving their field of expertise, including accounting, construction management, engineering, and law to join us. It was perfect timing. The stars were aligning to create another relationship out of South Florida that would end up challenging the integrity of every aspect of our strategies and ultimately doubling the size of the business.

THE ULTIMATE TEST

I have witnessed the life-changing benefits for thousands of clients in every imaginable demographic who have used The Perpetual Wealth Strategy.

The strategy is ideal for those in the middle of their career and for building assets with cash flow. However, it is equally ideal for those who are within 15 years or less of what is typically referred to as "retirement age." The strategy can accelerate the time frame for retirement, but also, because of our philosophy and education, alter the very notion of retirement.

Paradigm Life is a virtual business, which means that we rarely meet with clients in our physical office. Our model consists of consultations and education done through webinars and online video meetings. Additionally, our website has thousands of hours of online video tutorials and courses, so anyone can learn about what we do. We can do business in every state and Canada as well.

Therefore, it's not uncommon to meet with and teach intriguing people with diverse backgrounds, like Tim.

TIM FROM AFRICA

In 2011, Tim contacted me and requested that we schedule a time to meet. What I assumed was going to be a routine one-on-one webinar turned into a friendship, a professional relationship, and the most rigorous test of the strategy to date.

Tim had worked with another one of the handful of professionals who advocate what Paradigm Life does. Not entirely happy with the ongoing support he was getting, he began using the resources on our website to further his education. He reached out to me and we hit it off. Tim was originally from Western Canada but had grown up in Africa, where his parents were Christian missionaries.

One day, Tim said to me, with sort of a chuckle, "Hey, you're not going to believe this."

"What?"

"So, I just subscribed to this new financial newsletter, and one of their first pieces talked about why the only life insurance you should buy is term insurance and to stay away from cash value insurance."

"OK," I responded, a bit confused. "I'm not surprised—that's what everyone says."

"I know. That's not what I was trying to say." Tim was clearly excited about something. "I actually wrote them and told them about The Perpetual Wealth Strategy and what you do. The editor wrote back. He told me that they would commission me to write an editorial brief on the whole thing."

"Really? That sounds cool," I responded, not knowing the extent of the opportunity.

"No, you don't get it, Pat." Tim was getting a little nervou_ "This conservative financial newsletter was started by really reputable guys; these guys know their stuff." Now he was really starting to sound anxious.

"Are you going to do it?" I asked, trying to sound encouraging.

"Yeah, but I don't know where to start." I could hear the last bit of air come out of his sail of excitement.

"Don't worry man, I'm here for you. I can help you through the entire thing," I said.

For months, Tim and I dug in for a deep dive into every aspect of our strategy. Questions came up that I hadn't ever been asked. Tim attended the Truth Concepts software training in Houston with me and got an even more comprehensive picture there.

After what seemed like a lifetime, his piece was complete, and he sent it off.

At the time, Tim was working for a small company in Atlanta as a controller in their accounting department. He was doing well, had a young family, and would never have imagined the result of a simple inquiry and subsequent challenge of authoring a research brief. Tim was ultimately offered a full-time position at this new pub-

ny. He ended up combining the wisdom
al analysts and writers to create the most
e educational program on insurance-centric
egy ever. Since 2011, if you have come across
material referencing the Income for Life, 770 Account,
702(j), President's Account, or 501(k) strategies, it originated from the team at the Palm Beach Letter, now called
the Palm Beach Research Group (palmbeachgroup.com).

Although Tim's research was compelling, Tyson, the editor
of the newsletter at the time, dove in and verified the
legitimacy of what Tim had so tirelessly compiled.

TYSON FROM ENGLAND

Tyson's interest was like that of the many business owners
and executives who recognize that the best return on
investment will never come from a mutual fund, rental
property, or stock. They themselves will always produce
the greatest return.

That's why Tyson and his newsletter subscribers gravitated toward the strategy. They know, deep-down, that
they and their businesses are their most valuable asset.
They understand the importance of asset protection and a
secure location for their cash assets. Tax efficiency is also
a priority, because the less they pay in tax, the more they
must invest in themselves and their business. Additionally,

they want a return on their money that's comparable to a retirement plan. For business owners, however, one of the most attractive benefits of the strategy is that they can borrow from the insurance company against their liquid cash, guaranteed.

I still remember the first call I had with Tyson. His confidence in speaking, in his charming British accent, about anything that had to do with money, was immediately conveyed. My normal position for a phone call is on my wireless headset, hands behind my head, staring at the ceiling while sitting on the worn love seat in my office. That position only lasted a minute during that first call. I knew almost immediately that the call was going to test me. I was on my feet in a hurry, pacing the room while answering and verifying questions and statements for about an hour. The call concluded with Tyson wanting to not only write more about what we do but also to become a Paradigm client. He started accounts for himself and his wife and eventually opened multiple accounts for himself and his kids, too.

Tyson has a vast experience analyzing investment strategies and writing about them, which gave him firsthand experience with the risk associated with most investing. The benefits of our strategy—such as tax-free guaranteed growth, privacy, and liquidity using the loan provision—were becoming clearer to him. But no one knew investing better than Mark, his partner in the Palm Beach Letter.

MEETING MARK

I was planning a family Christmas visit to Pompano Beach that winter. That's not very far from the Palm Beach Letter office, so Tyson and I agreed to meet up in person. We had lunch, and he told me more about his business, his experience in the financial world, and what he was planning for this new publishing venture. Then, in what seemed to be on impulse, Tyson suggested that we go see Mark at his office. Up to that time, I knew Mark by his pen name, Michael Masterson, who was a highly regarded author and businessperson in the publishing community.

His office was straight out of a movie. The beauty of South Florida in December was breathtaking, especially given the contrasting wintery weather back home in the mountains of Utah. The air was 75 degrees; it was sunny, and a light breeze barely moved the leaves of the thick palm trees that surrounded the unassuming building. A vintage sports car stood out front.

As we walked in, his secretary greeted us in a perfectly manicured waiting room, adorned with shelves of Mark's books. His office was at the other end of the building. The walk to reach it seemed to last for half an hour. The uniqueness of Mark's office would make anyone stare. In one part of the spacious room was an art studio, with completed works on the wall and an easel holding a painting in progress. There was a pool table, a sitting area, and a massage table. As we crossed the threshold into his office, the décor made it seem like you were transported back in time. As I sat in awe, I noticed there was still a faint scent of cigar smoke in the air. Before I knew it, Tyson interrupted my daydream.

"Mark, this is Patrick from Utah. Patrick, tell Mark what you do."

I tried not to look startled at the on-the-spot request, even though the blood in my body seemed to rush to my face. I stammered out—appropriate to the entire experience—an impulsive response describing the uniqueness of the strategy, some of the high-level characteristics, and how I originally connected with Tim. I was met with the pushback and skepticism you would expect from someone who has been pitched every financial strategy under the sun. It was an enlightening few hours.

A SHIFT TO SOLID GROUND

My experience that day solidified in me the importance of highlighting the more intriguing aspects of the strategy for individuals building wealth. It also made me realize the importance of teaching and illustrating how those who had already amassed wealth can also benefit to the same degree.

For someone who's 55 to 65 years old, planning retirement

the typical way is getting riskier every year. If you look at the recommended distribution rates for a market-based portfolio, both inside and outside of a government-qualified plan such as a 401(k), you're looking at 3.5 to a maximum 4 percent distribution rate. What that means is that someone with a million dollars in their retirement account is being told by financial advisors that they can only take out $40,000 a year if they don't want to run out of money. They may be a millionaire, but at that level, they can't live off the cash flow it's producing. The Perpetual Wealth Strategy for someone in this stage of life can significantly increase not only the rate at which cash flow distribution is recommended, but also provide peace of mind through an income that lasts as long as you live.

Using this approach means it is not only possible but imperative to take back control of your financial future. If you don't control your wealth, then Wall Street, banks, and the government will. But they're poor stewards of our money. They don't represent values and principles—they represent profits. Too often, our protection and our certainty are sacrificed in favor of their gain.

The Perpetual Wealth Strategy means storing your wealth with a mutual insurance company in a uniquely structured life insurance policy. The financing needs you experience in your life, such as buying a car or a home, are then covered by a provision of your policy that allows you to borrow from the insurance company against the equity that you're building. It's simple, straightforward, and safe.

THE ELEVATION GROUP

When I first started Paradigm Life, the socioeconomic spectrum of clients I worked with was confined to a somewhat narrow range. In 2012, a highly regarded CPA named Tom Wheelwright was instrumental in broadening that range and teaching me how to make a bigger impact in people's lives by improving my teaching quality as well as teaching me higher-level financial and tax concepts used by the wealthy.

On the 2012 Real Estate Guys Investor Summit at Sea, I reconnected with Tom, whom I had been acquainted with in the past. That year of the summit, Robert Kiyosaki—author and investor, best known for his book *Rich Dad Poor Dad*—was the headlining faculty member. Accompanying Kiyosaki were his personal advisors, called Rich Dad Advisors, which included Tom, the expert on tax and wealth strategy.

Among CPAs, some just do your taxes; others advise you on what to do with your money, which usually focuses on how to save the most now on your taxes, with little regard for future consequences. Tom's firm, Wealthability, takes a different approach. They work primarily with entrepreneurs, business owners, and investors and provide them with education and strategy to live tax-free.

Tom was also part of an organization called The Elevation Group that had created a popular online financial education program with tens of thousands of participants.

Tom informed them of what Paradigm Life did, and they wanted to add it as part of their growing curriculum. A few months later, toward the end of 2012, I flew down to Austin, Texas, to officially meet the group and film the initial video tutorials.

From there, I had the experience of a lifetime. I hosted several webinars for them, recorded dozens of educational videos, and worked with thousands of their members from all over the country. I learned directly from Tom about new ways to think about taxes, interest rates, debt, business, and real estate that I could not only apply to the new clients I was working with but also to my more established clients.

Heads I Win, Tails You Lose and the accompanying resource, *The Financial Strategy Study Guide* (headsortailsiwin.com/StudyGuide), are the culmination of philosophy, perspective, guidance, financial strategies and tactics, motivation, and inspiration based on these experiences and many more, to teach you how to regain control of your wealth and achieve financial freedom.

KEY TAKEAWAYS

- Regain control of your finances—if you don't, someone else will.
- Learn how to think for yourself.
- The Perpetual Wealth Strategy means storing your wealth with a mutual insurance company in a uniquely structured life insurance policy.
- The Perpetual Wealth Strategy has multiple applications and can be utilized by clients in various walks, circumstances, and phases of life.
- An investment in you will always create the greatest rate of return.

CHAPTER 3

QUESTION EVERYTHING

"What we observe is not nature itself, but nature exposed to our method of questioning."

—WERNER HEISENBERG

The great American labyrinth begins while you're still in high school, where you're taught the following:

1. Go to college because college leads to a career with healthcare and retirement benefits. College is expensive, but there are student loans available that will pay for the whole thing.

2. After your 30-year career, you don't have to work anymore and should retire. To retire, you are told a 401(k) account with mutual funds as investments is the way to go and that the government will provide you with Social Security income during retirement on top of that.

3. When you have the means necessary, you should buy a house and put at least 20 percent toward the purchase. You are told to pay the mortgage loan from the bank off as soon as possible and even consider a 15-year loan to do it quicker. Your real estate agent has taught you well, and you firmly believe, as she does, that your home eventually becomes your most valuable asset.
4. A new vehicle must occupy the new garage of your new home, and because of your great credit score, you can qualify for a zero-percent automobile loan.
5. When your bank account gets a little thin from payments going to income taxes, health insurance, your 401(k) account, Social Security and Medicare taxes, and the bank who gave you a student loan, mortgage, and car loan, don't worry!
6. Credit cards will give you points and rewards!

This is the vicious cycle that most Americans find themselves in. The empirical data evidenced in the introduction tells a story that conventional wisdom isn't that wise and that this route may not be the best course of action for everyone.

These social beliefs and expectations are not as realistic as they seem.

WHO'S TEACHING YOU?

The people who are telling you that this is the way to use your money wisely are those who have the most to gain. They're looking out for themselves, not for you. Everything financial advisors are taught goes to confirm the standard narrative.

Look at the college loan industry. The higher education lobby is huge. If those government-backed college loans went away, what would happen? The college business model, especially the for-profit model, would be destroyed. Tuition would drop. All that investment in new buildings and other ways to attract students would be lost.

Look at banks. Banks control everything, and they spend vast sums on advertising and promotion and lobbying for their benefit. They work hard to convince you that you should borrow for everything and keep your savings with them.[19]

"Unburdened with the experience of the past, each generation of bankers believes that it knows best, and each generation produces some who have to learn the hard way."

—IRVINE SPRAGUE, FORMER CHAIRMAN OF THE FEDERAL DEPOSIT INSURANCE CORPORATION

Wall Street has taken over the massive amounts invested

---

19   https://hbr.org/2014/06/the-price-of-wall-streets-power

in 401(k) mutual funds. The amount spent on lobbying and advertising and promotion is enormous—the financial lobby alone is an $8 billion industry.[20] It all goes to convince you that this is the way financial planning is done, that your 401(k) is the best way to save for retirement, and that the best way to build that retirement fund is to invest it with them.

Look closer at consumer credit and lending. Huge amounts of money are spent to advertise and promote credit cards, car loans, and mortgages. Rationally, you should step back and think, "If they're spending so much on TV commercials and celebrity spokespeople, they must be making a lot of money off these products. Where is all the profit coming from?" It's coming from the high interest rates and fees that they never really tell you about until you're already signed up.

Everything in our economy today is leveraged. Let's say that mortgages were outlawed. You would have to significantly reduce the price of your house to sell it, because no one could afford the cash up front to buy it. But because mortgages do exist, you don't have to come up with the entire balance, which increases the price of homes. Same thing with cars. If you had to buy a car with cash, hardly anybody could. Everything in our economy is priced with leverage, even the stock market. At the same time, we're

20   http://www.opensecrets.org/lobby/top.php?indexType=c&showYear=a

all taught to pay off debt, to get out of debt, to be debt-free. In fact, that's not a good thing to do, because you're battling everything else that is priced with debt factored in. That's why people always find themselves in bad situations.

THE TYPICAL MINDSET

The result of following the typical mindset about your finances is that Wall Street and the banking industry get bigger and bigger. Any gains you might have made on your investments are wiped out during the inevitable downturns in their cycles, fees and commissions, and inflation. People continue to follow the typical approach to their money because of the sheer number of those doing the exact same thing and thinking that any alternative is too risky. People are naturally trusting, and they trust the crowd's opinion of financial markets and the conventional wisdom of investment, debt, and retirement. The typical models don't work.

Banks and Wall Street are collecting your money for retirement savings in one hand and lending you back the same money at higher interest rates with the other hand. All the money you're investing in mutual funds earns some money, but the earnings are offset by the interest and fees you pay when you borrow the same money at higher interest rates.

The numbers are staggering. Mortgage debt is more than $15 trillion,[21] consumer credit is almost $4 trillion,[22] auto loan debt is $1.1 trillion,[23] and student loan debt is $1.5 trillion.[24] That much money in debt is hard to fathom.

What will it take for people to wake up to this?

CONTROL = FREEDOM

When you control your money and financial potential, you are truly free. The biggest step to financial freedom is to consider yourself your most valuable asset, not your 401(k), home, an investment property, or your bank account. When you adopt this mindset, you start to think differently about how you dress and groom yourself, how well you maintain your body, how you treat other people, and how you look for opportunities—how to be more valuable to your employer, your colleagues, your children, and yourself.

If you don't have control of your money right now, that means the control is with someone else. Who is that someone else? It's someone who didn't earn the money that you're investing with them. It's someone who is managing

21 https://www.federalreserve.gov/data/mortoutstand/current.htm

22 https://www.federalreserve.gov/releases/g19/current/default.htm

23 https://www.federalreserve.gov/releases/g19/current/default.htm

24 https://www.federalreserve.gov/releases/g19/current/default.htm

a lot of other money from other people as well. Do you really think that the mutual fund manager who's taking care of your 401(k) account is thinking, "What can I do with [insert your name]'s money that's in their personal best interest?" No. That person is thinking, "How can I make the most money for me? How can I hit my bonus this quarter?"

At the banks and financial firms, collectively they think, "We're a public company. We need to hit our quarterly projections. If that means individual account holders suffer, too bad." Everybody's pressured to grow, grow, grow, grow—at your expense.

You're putting control of your financial future in the hands of people who don't have your best interests in mind. You're relinquishing control to big institutions that serve their own needs first and yours a distant second. You're increasing your risk while minimizing the earnings on your money. The typical financial mindset benefits institutions, not you.

When your money is tied up in funds managed by big institutions, you're not prepared for large expenses, layoffs, emergencies, or market downturns. A 401(k)-based investment and retirement plan was never intended to be the "American Way to Financial Freedom." Today, the deck is stacked against most Americans, and it will be too late to make the course corrections necessary. When you consider fund manager performance over time, fund and administrator fees, and back-end taxes upon withdrawal, the 401(k) looks like the best retirement plan *only* for Uncle Sam and the financial institutions. Then you take into consideration the increases in life expectancies, caps on contributions, and falling retirement account distribution rates. The 401(k) makes no sense.

Most people still consider a million dollars a lot of money. Let's say that you amassed this sum in your portfolio and were ready to retire. According to renowned financial analyst Dr. Wade Pfau, columnist for the *Wall Street Journal* and *Forbes,* the maximum rate of distribution today, based on low interest rates and volatility, is 3.5 percent per year for 20 years.[25] That means that you can withdraw $35,000 per year for 20 years and be certain that you won't run out of money. That $35,000 is before taxes. Depending on your tax bracket—let's assume a blended rate of 20 percent—that ends up as $28,000 in spendable income. How is anyone supposed to live off that? If you go to headsortailsiwin.com/StudyGuide, I recorded a tutorial that takes you step by step through the math and actual fund performance. You will see more clearly how unlikely the feat of a million dollars is when considering taxes, fees, and inflation. If you have the typical mindset,

---

25 https://www.forbes.com/sites/wadepfau/2015/05/13/improving-retirement-outcomes-with-investments-life-insurance-and-income-annuities/#5305c35737ab

you're handing over pretty much everything to others. You're obligating yourself to debt, because when all your money is in your investment account or retirement savings, you're not able to spend it. You're pushed into using expensive consumer credit.

You're also obligating yourself to a tax code that can change. The widely held assumption of typical retirement specialists is that you'll be in a lower income tax bracket when you retire. That's risky. You're basically wagering that your tax rate is either going to be the same or better than the tax rate when you put the money in today.

You're tying up money until you're of retirement age. But what if you need the money before then? What if you have an emergency, medical expense, or you get laid off and you can't find a job for a year? If you need to tap that retirement money, you have to pay taxes and get slapped with a penalty.

What if you want to tap your 401(k) to pay a child's college tuition? You don't want your child to have to go into debt, but tapping your own money could wipe out well over a million dollars of retirement money because of opportunity costs and lost interest.

All the retirement models assume you'll be willing and able to work until you're 65. But in today's economy, you might find yourself pushed out of the workforce at 55. You might never find another job as good. That affects your retirement—and because the likelihood of living into our 80s is now higher, that means even less.

At the same time, Social Security funds are steadily depleting. According to a study by the Social Security Administration, the disability fund is going to run out in 2028,[26] and Social Security by 2034.[27] Social Security and Medicare have huge unfunded liabilities coming up. If you're betting on Social Security to provide for or supplement your retirement, you're in for a rude awakening.

RESISTING THE PRESSURE

People feel powerful pressure to put their retirement funds into 401(k) plans and take the employer match. That advice can be misleading. You're not really getting a 100 percent match from your employer. The maximum amount you can contribute to a 401(k) is determined by the government; match programs are typically based on a percentage of your earned income. Most employers only match, up to a point, what you put in—and your employer doesn't have to match your contribution at all. An employer can choose not to contribute, and you have no recourse.

26   https://www.ssa.gov/policy/trust-funds-summary.html

27   http://time.com/money/4213065/will-social-security-run-out-money/

Most people don't really think about this. They contribute as much as they can and trust that it will all work out. They prefer the payroll deduction approach, so they don't have to think about it. That's what they've been taught: you're not disciplined or educated enough to save and invest money.

There's a problem with that approach. The majority of the $100 trillion[28] in American wealth is in Wall Street's hands. According to Dalbar Research—which analyzes investor *actual* returns—over the last 15 years, the average asset allocation fund investor has earned 2.58 percent; equity fund investors have earned 5.29 percent.[29] This is before fees and taxes.

If returns are so poor for 401(k) plans, why do people continue to participate in them?

It's human nature. Everybody else is doing it, right? You don't want to be the odd person out. Doing something different isn't natural. It makes you feel unsafe. It's the status quo, and change in the status quo comes only with severe pain. The pain of changing is less than the pain of staying the same.

---

lso all just busy. We work hard, we need time for nilies, and we don't want to take on more tasks and responsibilities. We don't want to take the time and mental energy to learn something, especially if it's not pressing to our well-being. It's just easier to sign up for the 401(k) automatic payroll deductions. Looking at alternatives that might be better is just too much work.

A DIFFERENT WAY

It takes a certain type of person to realize the problems with American personal finance, dominated by the 401(k) mutual fund and banking industry. These problems are real and need to be challenged. Not everyone is ready to believe me, but as George Washington said,

> "Truth will ultimately prevail where there are pains to bring it to light."

Those pains are on the foreseeable horizon. You can take steps and find solutions now. If you are the sort of person who wants to regain control of their future, achieve financial freedom, and live a life you love, keep reading. I'm going to tell you about a different way. It's simpler, it's safer, and it's historically proven. It will reduce your anxieties about money once and for all and allow you to be more productive. It's the route taken by far fewer people, but isn't success normally that way?

KEY TAKEAWAYS

- You are truly free when you take control of your money and financial potential.
- When you take the biggest step to financial freedom and consider yourself your most valuable asset, it changes how you think about everything.
- Resist the pressure to rely on conventional financial advice and educate yourself.
- You are the source of financial freedom, not a college degree, secure job, or 401(k).

CHAPTER 4

BREAK AWAY FROM WALL STREET

"Corporations and Wall Street in pursuit of short-term profits have given the economy away."

—PAUL CRAIG ROBERTS

Wall Street isn't simply the New York Stock Exchange and the surrounding financial companies that share the same neighborhood. Wall Street refers to the financial business in general, whether that be investment banks, stock exchanges, stock brokerages, or investment companies. They have the largest influence in the world, and no matter the circumstances, they always seem to wind up on top. For each of the last three decades, their influential clout has grown. Despite their continual scandals, market manipulations, booms, busts, and eventual bailouts, they are still trusted to be stewards over most Americans' savings.

Wall Street's typical financial advice was called into question once again during the 2008-2010 meltdown. Although many alternative investments, strategies, and tactics became popular and available, most people still hang onto one of the strongest bonds I have ever seen: Wall Street and their retirement plan.

QUESTION THE EXPERTS

The reason for the bond is that we tend to make decisions about a person based on their reputation or how credible they seem, rather than understanding what they're talking about. Look at Alan Greenspan. Known as "The Maestro," he was the longest-standing chairman of the Board of Governors of the Federal Reserve System. Greenspan testified before Congress numerous times, both during his tenure and after. Until the financial crisis, rarely did anybody question his tactics for fear of looking incompetent.

Most people trust those who are deemed competent. We assume that if someone wears a nice suit and sounds credible, they're going to do the right thing. But as Warren Buffet once said, "Only when the tide goes out do you discover who's been swimming naked."

> *"The sound banker, alas, is not one who foresees danger and avoids it. But one who, when he is ruined, is ruined in a conventional and orthodox way, along with his fellows, so that no one can really blame him."*
>
> —JOHN MAYNARD KEYNES

During the financial crisis, that unguarded trust became apparent as the shady business practices of many firms were exposed. Here are a few examples:

- 2009, Bernie Madoff's $65 billion Ponzi scheme.
- 2009, Allen Stanford gathered $8 billion in a Ponzi scheme by falsely promising the safety and security of certificates of deposit.
- 2010, Chase, GMAC, Bank of America, and others were caught performing nonjudicial foreclosures.
- 2010, Countrywide's CEO Angelo Mozilo misrepresented company data to appease investors. These investors consisted of many Americans who held mutual funds or had pensions.
- 2012, several investment firms, including Chase and Barclays, were intentionally manipulating LIBOR, a benchmark interest rate, affecting trillions of dollars of loans.
- 2012, HSBC was caught money laundering for Mexican drug cartels and countries known to shelter terrorists, such as Iran.

More recently, even as the tide seems to be approaching heightened levels and not receding, the poor fiduciary stewardship of many financial firms continues to be exposed. Just consider the recent event with Wells Fargo.

In 2016, we learned that over 5,000 Wells Fargo employees were knowingly involved in opening more than 3.5 million fake bank accounts. That means 5,000 employees thought it was perfectly okay to create fraudulent accounts to inflate performance numbers.

A company that does the right thing often has to make decisions that don't benefit them, like issuing a recall or firing a chief executive. The financial industry, however, is focused on quarterly earnings and yearly bonuses, which makes them willing to sacrifice the long term for short-term gains. Wall Street has become a monstrosity that manipulates the American public and saddles them with the bill. The massive fines that are paid reduce shareholder value. Bailouts and government intervention result in higher taxes and/or inflation.

THE REALITY OF PASSIVE INVESTMENT

Markets are not inherently sinister, but they can easily be manipulated and typically are—and not in your favor. Unless you've been educated to understand how this happens, you can get hurt when you invest. The market is not a place for your savings. If you know what you're doing as well as understand how to make good investments and how to hedge your risk, you're the exception.

Even experienced people who work in finance don't have full knowledge about how everything works. Sophisticated investors do understand Wall Street, but most people don't know what mutual funds they own or what stocks and bonds are in that mutual fund. They don't know what the end game is and what they should do in retirement.

One of the many things I teach our clients is how the market works from a mathematical perspective.

A common misconception in the narrative of typical financial planning is compound interest. The typical financial planner will state that over the last 20 to 30 years, the market has grown by a certain percent every year. This number is what they use to project what a portfolio balance might look like in the future.

Let's dissect this simply. From 1998 to 2017—a period of 20 years—the S&P 500 index earned an average rate of return of 6.78 percent according to Pinnacle Data Corp.[30]

---

30   https://pinnacledata2.com/

AVERAGE ROR	6.78%
Year	S&P 500 Without Dividends
1998	26.69%
1999	19.51%
2000	(10.14%)
2001	(13.04%)
2002	(23.37%)
2003	26.38%
2004	8.99%
2005	3.00%
2006	13.62%
2007	3.53%
2008	(38.49%)
2009	23.45%
2010	12.78%
2011	(0.003%)
2012	13.41%
2013	29.60%
2014	11.39%
2015	(0.73%)
2016	9.54%
2017	19.42%

What does this mean?

The average American doesn't really know. They see these numbers and erroneously conclude that if they had money in the stock market, their wealth would grow by 6.78 percent yearly.

Using that logic, a $100,000 investment would turn into $371,363 over 20 years.

Present Value:	100,000
Annual Payment:	0.00
Annual Int. Rate:	6.78%
Years:	20
Future Value:	371,363

That's a lot of money, but it's not how the market works. If that $100,000 were invested in the S&P for 20 years, that's not what it would have earned.

Markets don't operate on a straight line and never have. They have good years and they have bad years. Yet somehow the narrative concludes that they miraculously end up all balancing out to a simple equation.

This next part is where most people tune out, but it's exactly where you should be paying close attention.

If you started with $100,000 at the beginning of 1998 and cashed out at the end of 2017, your balance would be $275,508—almost $100,000 less than what the average would have been.

Why?

Because markets fluctuate. When there's a loss, a subsequent gain must be much higher to balance out the loss. If you lost 10 percent on a $100,000 investment, your balance would be $90,000. To make up the loss and get back to break-even, you would have to earn 11.1 percent, not simply 10 percent. That's because if you lose 10 percent one year and then gain 10 percent the next, your average return over the two years is zero percent.

The chart shows the *actual* return on that $100,000 investment. It's really 5.20 percent—and that's gross, before fees.

Average Return: 6.78%		Actual Return: 5.20%		
Year	Beg. of Year Acct. Value	Earnings Rate	Interest Earnings	End of Year Acct. Value
1998	100,000	26.69%	26,685	126,685
1999	126,685	19.51%	24,717	151,402
2000	151,402	(10.14%)	(15,351)	136,051
2001	136,051	(13.04%)	(17,741)	118,310
2002	118,310	(23.37%)	(27,648)	90,663
2003	90,663	26.38%	23,917	114,580
2004	114,580	8.99%	10,305	124,580
2005	124,885	3.00%	3,748	128,633
2006	128,633	13.62%	17,519	146,152
2007	146,152	3.53%	5,159	151,310
2008	151,310	(38.49%)	(58,233)	93,077
2009	93,077	23.45%	21,831	114,908
2010	114,908	12.78%	14,688	129,596
2011	129,596	(0.003%)	(4)	129,592
2012	129,592	13.41%	17,373	146,965
2013	146,965	29.60%	43,503	190,468
2014	190,468	11.39%	21,696	212,164
2015	212,164	(0.73%)	(1,542)	210,622
2016	210,622	9.54%	20,083	230,705
2017	230,705	19.42%	44,803	275,508
Totals		6.78%	175,508	275,508

One of the primary purposes of the S&P 500 is to give individuals a benchmark for performance of their specific set of funds and to give fund managers a target for performance.

According to Investopedia and other sources, more than 80 percent of fund managers *underperform* the S&P 500.[31]

Even Warren Buffet's Berkshire Hathaway has failed to beat the index since 2008.[32]

When you factor in the fee structure, which is how the fund manager is paid, the results worsen. When the management fee is just 1 percent, the balance erodes to $225,340, or a 4.15 percent return.

31   https://www.marketwatch.com/story/why-way-fewer-actively-managed-funds-
      beat-the-sp-than-we-thought-2017-04-24; https://www.investopedia.com/news/
      indexing-beats-active-management-bear-market/; https://www.investopedia.com/articles/
      investing/091015/statistical-look-passive-vs-active-management.asp; https://www.cnbc.
      com/2017/04/12/bad-times-for-active-managers-almost-none-have-beaten-the-market-over-
      the-past-15-years.html

32   https://seekingalpha.com/article/4150977-pretty-picture-buffett-vs-s-and-p-500

	Average Return: 6.78%			Actual Return: 4.15%	
Year	Beg. of Year Acct. Value	Earnings Rate	Interest Earnings	Misc. Fees	End of Year Acct. Value
1998	100,000	26.69%	26,685	(1,267)	125,418
1999	125,418	19.51%	24,470	(1,499)	148,389
2000	148,389	(10.14%)	(15,045)	(1,333)	132,101
2001	132,010	(13.04%)	(17,214)	(1,148)	113,649
2002	113,649	(23.37%)	(26,558)	(871)	86,220
2003	86,220	26.38%	22,745	(1,090)	107,875
2004	107,875	8.99%	9,702	(1,176)	116,401
2005	116,401	3.00%	3,493	(1,199)	118,685
2006	118,695	13.62%	16,166	(1,349)	133,512
2007	133,512	3.53%	4,712	(1,382)	136,842
2008	136,842	(38.49%)	(52,665)	(842)	83,336
2009	83,336	23.45%	19,546	(1,029)	101,853
2010	101,853	12.78%	13,020	(1,149)	113,723
2011	113,723	(0.003%)	(4)	(1,137)	112,583
2012	112,583	13.41%	15,092	(1,277)	126,398
2013	126,398	29.60%	37,415	(1,638)	162,176
2014	162,176	11.39%	18,473	(1,806)	178,842
2015	178,842	(0.73%)	(1,299)	(1,775)	175,767
2016	175,767	9.54%	16,759	(1,925)	190,601
2017	190,601	19.42%	37,015	(2,276)	225,340
Totals		6.78%	152,508	(27,168)	225,340

According to the Investment Company Institute, over $20 trillion is invested in 20,000 different funds. There are studies that state the average equity mutual fund fee structure is 1.28 percent;[33] however, many are charging more than 9 percent.[34]

The typical financial mindset would also stress the idea of a concept called *dollar cost averaging*, which simply means that they make ongoing contributions to the fund,

---

33   https://www.ici.org/pdf/2017_factbook.pdf

34   https://www.forbes.com/sites/kennethkim/2016/09/24/how-much-do-mutual-funds-really-cost/#35da484ea527; https://seekingalpha.com/article/4134452-avoid-worst-style-mutual-funds-q417

not simply a lump sum of money at the start. That does make a difference, but less than it seems.

At a $10,000 annual contribution and a 1 percent fee structure, the ending balance would be $369,257, for a 5.53 *actual* rate of return.

Year	Beg. of Year Acct. Value	Earnings Rate	Annual Savings	Interest Earnings	Misc. Fees	End of Year Acct. Value
Average Return: 6.78%				Actual Return: 5.53%		
1998		26.69%	10,000	2,669	(127)	12,542
1999	12,542	19.51%	10,000	4,398	(269)	26,670
2000	26,670	(10.14%)	10,000	(3,718)	(330)	32,623
2001	32,623	(13.04%)	10,000	(5,558)	(371)	36,694
2002	36,694	(23.37%)	10,000	(10,912)	(358)	35,425
2003	35,425	26.38%	10,000	11,983	(574)	56,834
2004	56,834	8.99%	10,000	6,011	(728)	72,116
2005	72,116	3.00%	10,000	2,464	(846)	83,735
2006	83,735	13.62%	10,000	12,766	(1,065)	105,436
2007	105,436	3.53%	10,000	4,074	(1,195)	118,315
2008	118,315	(38.49%)	10,000	(49,383)	(789)	78,143
2009	78,143	23.45%	10,000	20,673	(1,088)	107,728
2010	107,728	12.78%	10,000	15,049	(1,328)	131,449
2011	131,449	(0.003%)	10,000	(4)	(1,414)	140,030
2012	140,030	13.41%	10,000	20,113	(1,701)	168,441
2013	168,441	29.60%	10,000	52,821	(2,313)	228,949
2014	228,949	11.39%	10,000	27,218	(2,662)	263,505
2015	263,505	(0.73%)	10,000	(1,987)	(2,715)	268,802
2016	268,802	9.54%	10,000	26,584	(3,054)	302,332
2017	302,332	19.42%	10,000	60,655	(3,730)	369,257
Totals		6.78%	200,000	195,914	(26,657)	369,257

This analysis doesn't include taxes. The after-tax return would differ depending on whether the funds are held inside or outside a qualified plan like a 401(k).

Is this rate of return worth the risk required to earn it? Of course not, but the variable that enables an informed decision is usually not present—financial education. You are becoming educated, and as a result, can make more informed decisions instead of trusting others who seem competent.

The fact is that people trust financial advisors, stock brokers, and bankers because they seem to know what they're doing and say they have your best interests at heart. They trust that following their advice and putting their money into the usual investment vehicles is the right thing to do because everybody else is doing it. They make you feel good about being responsible and putting money away for retirement.

WALL STREET ISN'T WHAT IT USED TO BE

"Wall Street people learn nothing and forget everything."

—BENJAMIN GRAHAM

I witness the power and influence of Wall Street daily through interaction with clients and what I pay attention to in the media. Tens of trillions of dollars flow daily[35] in and out of their hands affording them an influence that is evident in advertising, lobbying, and politics. Surprisingly, it wasn't until the 1980s that they became a superpower. Coincidentally, that was the time period when the notion of retirement was popularized, resulting in their role to facilitate investments inside retirement accounts.

---

35 https://www.newyorkfed.org/medialibrary/microsites/prc/files/PRC-Intraday-Liquidity-Flows-Report.pdf

Here's the story.

Before the advent of the 401(k) and other retirement accounts, not many people invested in mutual funds, stocks, or bonds. Financial strategy was largely savings, life insurance, annuities, or a pension.

After companies such as Studebaker and United Steel defaulted on their pension obligations in the 1960s, companies realized that the pensions they promised their workers had become a big liability on their balance sheets. They needed a way to move away from defined benefits plans, such as pensions, to defined contribution plans. In other words, they were looking for a way to shift the burden off their balance sheet and onto the employees. Enter the 401(k) plan.

As originally conceived, this section of the IRS code was created to help highly paid corporate executives shelter their bonuses from taxation. It was never meant to be used as a retirement plan or a way to own mutual funds. In the 1980s, however, the law was interpreted and modified in a way that let full-time employees fund retirement accounts with pre-tax dollars and matching employer contributions. Here was the ideal way for companies to remove the liability that came with offering a pension plan and still dangle the carrot of a retirement benefit. These plans became very popular.

Wall Street got involved by offering to invest that money for you in mutual funds, stocks, and other investment vehicles. From the 1980s through the 2000s, there was massive growth in the market, which sparked the interest of more people who wanted to ride the wave. Wall Street was quick to find profitable ways to take advantage of that need.

These are the roles they play.

If you contribute money to your company 401(k), it goes to a custodian who pools it with everyone else's money and then invests it into a mutual fund with a mutual fund manager. Instead of keeping that money on their books as a liability (because they owe that to you), the mutual fund invests it to turn it into an asset, aiming to make a return on it. Every time the fund buys or sells something for its portfolio, it pays fees, commissions, and taxes. Those get passed down to the mutual fund owner, which means they eventually get passed down to you and erode the overall gain.

The risk factor you are dealing with is a big disparity between risk and reward. We are taught that mutual funds for retirement are safe investments because of diversification. The history of market corrections has proven otherwise.

Despite the lack of mutual fund positive performance,

the narrative remains that if you want to retire, you must use mutual funds.

HOW WALL STREET MAKES MONEY

"Fees never sleep."

—WARREN BUFFET

You pay fees to the fund managers and traders. They have an incentive to manage your money in a way that maximizes their fees, not in a way that maximizes your return. Fees are an issue for 401(k) and IRA accounts, which are almost entirely invested in mutual funds. These accounts have a lot of fees, restrictions, and penalties.

In 2015, a surprising event took place at the Fortune 500 company Ameriprise, which has almost a trillion dollars in assets and produces a revenue of more than $12 billion a year:

The employees of Ameriprise—the same people who are instrumental in the success of the company—sued their own employer for the excessive fees of their own company's 401(k) plan. The lawsuit was settled for $27.5 million. That settlement money came from Ameriprise revenue, so they basically paid it from the fees they got from other plans.[36]

---

36   https://www.nytimes.com/2011/10/15/your-money/turning-a-lens-on-ameriprise-financial.html; http://www.investmentnews.com/article/20150326/FREE/150329942/ameriprise-to-pay-27-5-million-settlement-in-401-k-fiduciary-breach

Ameriprise boldly states on their website:

> Ameriprise is a trusted financial firm that empowers you to enjoy the full and rich life you've earned. Learn about our history of strength, stability, and putting clients first.[37]

Wall Street investments are not the only way to save and invest.

SO, WHAT'S THE PROBLEM WITH 401(K) PLANS?

401(k)s weren't created to be retirement plans. Despite that, they're the primary way most Americans save for retirement today.

Let's start with why this vehicle became the "Big Bang" of Wall Street.

If you're a bank or financial institution, what motivates you? These institutions have four rules:

1. Get money.
2. Get money as often as possible.
3. Keep the money for as long as possible.
4. Give as little of the money back as possible.

---

37 https://www.ameriprise.com/financial-planning/about/

As pensions became too much of a burden for companies, the 401(k) was the ideal alternative. It aligned with every motivation above.

1. GET MONEY

A successful financial exchange between two parties requires a mutually agreed upon outcome of both getting what they want. The participants in a 401(k) want financial benefits such as earnings, tax benefits, and the confidence that their money will grow sufficiently to provide for their expenses when they stop working.

A pension played this role previously, guaranteeing income for as long as the employee lived. When pensions were the only option for employers to incentivize their employees, that's what they had to offer. When the 401(k) arrived on the scene, it was the superior choice for the employer. They had less liability, less hassle, and the same promise of retirement to the employee.

Wall Street has done a phenomenal job convincing the American public of this now widely held narrative.

2. GET MONEY AS OFTEN AS POSSIBLE

In 1981, adjustments to the 401(k) section of the tax code allowed employees to make contributions through a payroll deduction. In 2006, through the Pension Protection Act legislation, employees were automatically signed up for the plan unless they manually opted out. Automatic contributions and enrollment greatly increased the amount of money put into 401(k)s.[38] They are getting money from people every payday.

3. KEEP THE MONEY FOR AS LONG AS POSSIBLE

Your money is tied up in these plans. You can't touch it without paying significant penalties until you retire or reach age 59½. If you're currently employed, no matter what your age, you can't withdraw at all. And if you stop working before age 59½ you can't touch it. If you change employers, you can roll it over, but you can't use it until you meet the employment or age requirements.

So, you have a big pot of money in your 401(k), but the only way to get to it involves paying penalties. These plans have the serious drawback of lacking liquidity.

The incentive to the employee is that they don't have to pay any taxes on their contributions or gains up to a determined limit.

---

38 http://www.millernash.com/pension-protection-act-of-2006-summary-of-automatic-enrollment-provisions-under-401k-403b-and-governmental-457b-plans-08-25-2006/

However, you will still have to pay taxes on that money when you withdraw it in the future.

From a tax perspective, this may make sense. If your tax rate now is more than your tax rate when you want to withdraw the money, deferring your income may save you some money. That ideal scenario isn't guaranteed. Your 401(k) is regulated by the tax code, which can and does change when new laws are enacted. If Congress decides the country needs more money, the tax code can change. The vast pool of 401(k) money makes a tempting tax target.

4. GIVE AS LITTLE OF THE MONEY BACK AS POSSIBLE

One of the main incentives to contribute to a 401(k)—to defer income taxes—becomes, oddly enough, the primary disincentive to withdraw from it: having to pay income taxes!

Additionally, income tax rates may be higher in the future than they were when you contributed. Here's why that is likely to happen.

Fiscally, the United States has seen better days. With the looming budget deficit sitting at tens of trillions of dollars and Social Security and Medicare obligations at more than double that each, the probable means of meeting these obligations is increased taxation.

David M. Walker, who served as Comptroller General of the United States from 1998 to 2008, has stated on many occasions the dire condition of these future obligations, mainly the deficit and healthcare expenses. He predicts taxes will rise 200 percent[39] from their levels today.

Although it is not certain, an increase in future taxes is a good bet.

The advent of the 401(k) as the primary retirement savings vehicle today was the unintended consequence of a financial advisor named Ted Benna. Benna was seeking a way to help executives defer end-of-year bonuses and never intended the 401(k) to be what it is today.

However, because it aligns perfectly with the four rules of financial institutions, it remains, despite its challenges, the go-to vehicle for Americans to secure their financial future. There will be a rude awakening.

I was fortunate to meet Ted Benna and even did a podcast with him. Check out headsortailsiwin.com/StudyGuide to listen to our conversation and learn more about the 401(k).

---

39 https://www.npr.org/2010/03/09/124460237/after-financial-ruin-plotting-americas-comeback

> *"It is well enough that people of the nation do not understand our banking and monetary system. For if they did, I believe there would be a revolution before tomorrow morning."*
>
> —HENRY FORD

I want you to think twice about the risks of the typical retirement investment system and consider a serious alternative to it.

KEY TAKEAWAYS

- Wall Street isn't what it used to be. The vast inflow of 401(k) money since the 1980s has made mutual funds very popular and incentivized fund managers to make money off fees and commissions. Those costs get passed down to you.
- The risk isn't worth the return. The money you put into your 401(k) is subject to market volatility, inflation, taxes, and fees, while returns on the investment are low.
- You don't have access to your investment until you retire or reach age 59-½. The lack of liquidity means you may need to go into debt even though you have a lot of money in your retirement account.
- Breaking away from the Wall Street mindset isn't easy. You must go against what everyone else is telling you to do and think for yourself.

CHAPTER 5

AVOIDING THE INVESTING AND LENDING TRAP

"A bank is a place that will lend you money if you can prove that you don't need it."

—BOB HOPE

My client James is a successful contractor who builds big structures like Target and Walmart stores. After the crash of 2008-2009, things went south in his industry.

He kept doing jobs and bidding on projects, trying to keep his construction crews busy. As a new source of business, he decided to look for dilapidated apartment complexes that he could buy, fix up, and then rent out. He knew there were a lot of complexes in foreclosure, owned by out-of-state people who had wanted to invest in real estate.

These buildings were usually priced at half-a-million to a million dollars. Because he understood construction, costs, and project management, he thought he would be a good operational risk from a bank's perspective. He was also a good financial risk, with a lot of money in the bank from both his business and personal accounts provable by his ledgers.

Even though he was requesting loans for less than what he had in the bank, the banks were giving him the runaround. The real estate market was crashing, so there was some understandable resistance and hesitancy by banks. They didn't want to lend to him because they were sticking to rigid guidelines instead of using common sense.

James got more and more frustrated with the whole lending system, which led him to learn about alternatives and, ultimately, to open insurance policies designed for high cash value. James began allocating his excess cash away from his bank and to the insurance company. This allowed him to increase the return of his reserves for his family and other businesses and to avoid the frustrations of dealing with a bank when he wanted a loan.

His new source of financing was the line of credit that

the insurance company gave him against his growing account value.

He used it to purchase the buildings and finance the improvements. Once a property was all remodeled and ready to go, his bank was willing to lend James the money. Of course, that was only after he'd done all the legwork and taken all the risks. He was able to secure conventional financing to pay off the loan from the insurance company, which freed up liquidity to fund his next deal.

The concept of using a loan to purchase investment real estate is also known as leverage. Using leverage increases your return on investment because when you acquire the property, you don't have to come up with 100 percent of the money. The bank loans the money to you and, in exchange, expects payments that include interest. A profitable investment is when the cash flow from the property is higher than the bank payment and the other operational expenses. Without bank financing, the typical real estate investment would require the entire purchase price as the investment.

The bank James had a relationship with required the property to be in a certain condition before they would lend him their money. Using a loan from the insurance company allowed James to acquire and rehabilitate the building to comply with the bank parameters.

The banking industry is dominant when it comes to loans. They control a lot of market share, which means they can choose when they want to take a risk. During and after the Great Recession, banks were being very conservative and risk-averse. They simply weren't lending. They're willing to accept your money and pay you almost nothing in interest, but when you want to borrow money to invest in your business, they aren't there for you.

> *"Banking is necessary; banks are not."*
>
> —BILL GATES

Both storing your money in a bank and asking a bank for a loan are inefficient and inflexible ways to manage your cash.

SAVING VS. INVESTING

"Savings and investment are indissolubly linked. It is impossible to encourage one and discourage the other."

—MURRAY ROTHBARD

Let's talk about the difference between saving and investing.

Saving is supposed to be the preservation of capital. With savings (ideally), you're not going to lose money. If you have a dollar now, and you put it into a savings account

in a bank, you're going to have a dollar tomor.
years from now. The saved money is guarantee
bank. It's not at risk, other than the bank's stabil
also liquid—you can take it out at any time. You get a   ,
and you're not likely to lose any principal.

Saving is about preserving money. Investing is about growing money, but it comes with risks—nothing is guaranteed. With investing, if you start with a dollar today, you might have $1.50 in a couple of years, or you might have only 50 cents.

A big dilemma with the US personal finance industry is that saving has now somehow morphed into investing. They're considered the same thing, but they're not.

Most people are confused about the definition of an investment. An investment to most people is:

- The stock market
- A mutual fund
- An exchange-traded fund
- A 401(k)
- An IRA
- A piece of real estate

The best investment strategy is to figure out a way to make another dollar, not give money to a stockbroker so that *they* could make you another dollar. The first one you have control over, the second you don't. If you want money to grow, you need to figure out how to do it with what you can control, like your business or an investment you understand. When you make a profit, *then* you can store the capital in savings.

I teach clients that once they have their reserve in place, typically six months of your earned income, the remaining amount is your opportunity fund. That's the money available to you to capitalize on ways to grow it—what most identify as an investment.

Investment covers not only how you grow your wealth, but also investments in yourself, like getting a certification, an education, advanced degrees, and improving upon or learning a new skill.

Maybe you have a passion for marketing, so you spend $5,000 for a marketing course. Soon that helps you become a marketing director, making $10,000 more per year than you were making before. That's a 100 percent return on your investment in the first year alone, and you have full control over it. One of the best ways to make more money (especially for people just starting out) is to invest in specialized education or other things that have a big value proposition and personal control.

I also think a business is one of the number one investments. Starting a business is how most people grow much of their wealth. Ironically, successful business owners fall into the same trap and end up gravitating toward typical financial planning and get their employees involved as well. What's one of the most popular benefits? Offering a 401(k) and matching employee contributions—an investment the business owner doesn't control. The business owner makes their own contributions, upwards of $35,000 to $40,000 per year, transferring money from a location they control to one they don't. Thankfully, the business owners reading this book will have a better way to save and grow their wealth that doesn't carry the risk and uncertainty that the typical strategy carries.

THE EXTINCTION OF SAVINGS

The traditional savings plan, until the advent of the 401(k), was cash value life insurance policies. People also had pensions, which are a combination of life insurance and an annuity. They were *saving* for their future. In the early 1980s, it started to change.

Pensions were true savings vehicles. A calculation of a percentage of an employee's salary was determined, and money was put aside by the company, the employee, or a combination of both. A pension was a contractual obligation that guaranteed a predetermined stream of income to an employee for the rest of their life unless the company or municipality went out of business or failed to fund or manage the pension money properly.

A pension and 401(k) plan work completely differently. A pension is based on actuarial science. You know how many people work at the company, you know how much each contributes to the pension fund and what their retirement benefit will be, you know how many will retire and when, and you know how long after retirement most will die. That tells you very precisely how much money the plan needs to have at any given time to meet its predetermined obligations to the retirees.

Typically, insurance companies would be delegated the responsibility to properly create the pension plan. However, the business world realized the opportunity for more revenue by administering the plans themselves. They started taking on the responsibility, but also the risk.

Those obligations placed a lot of liability on the company. Many companies went bankrupt because of the mismanagement of their pension funds, including American Airlines in 2005, Delphi Corporation in 2009, and Bethlehem Steel in 2001.[40]

The 401(k) was an ideal solution for companies.

40 https://www.nytimes.com/2005/10/30/magazine/the-end-of-pensions.html

A 401(k) is often described as the modern replacement for a pension, but it's not an equal replacement. A pension is a sure bet contractually, with a defined benefit paid out every month. A 401(k) doesn't guarantee anything.

A 401(k) doesn't guarantee the rate of return, fees, income, or the future balance. The money invested in a 401(k) could grow, but that's not a certainty—the stock market could crash, for instance. The tax benefits aren't guaranteed, either. The money you put into the 401(k) isn't taxed until you withdraw it, at which point your tax rate is presumably lower. But that's not a certainty, either; your biggest deductions are gone, such as mortgage interest and child credits, and tax rates can and do change—and so does your personal income.

INFLATION: THE INCONSPICUOUS EROSION OF WEALTH

"Inflation is as violent as a mugger, as frightening as an armed robber, and as deadly as a hit man."

—RONALD REAGAN

In my experience, inflation is one of the most misunderstood financial concepts. It is used in the financial media as if it were a naturally occurring phenomena, like cycles of the moon.

In 1971, President Nixon took the US dollar off the gold standard by ceasing the redemption of gold by foreign countries that traded with the US.

Today, our flexible monetary system permits a central bank, the Federal Reserve System, to add money to the system that wasn't there before. No value was created that warranted more money to exist. What ends up happening is like adding more water to a pitcher of Kool-Aid. There's more to drink, but the taste is diluted.

Inflation causes a general increase in prices and a fall in the purchasing value of money. One cause of inflation is having more money chasing the same amount of goods and services. The basic law of supply and demand means prices will rise.

Let's say the housing market is tight—lots of people want to buy a house, but not that many new houses are being built. The demand is high, the supply is low. House prices go up—and so do the prices of the things you need to build a house, like lumber. But that means the price of lumber goes up for everyone—not just house builders. That's inflation. The cost of just about everything rises over time, because rising wages and cycles of supply and demand mean prices will always slowly go up. Sometimes inflation can rise sharply, however, and prices for goods and services rise sharply as well.

If you sock away money into a long-term investment, you have no idea what that money's going to be worth by the time you're able to use it, because you can't fully predict the rate of inflation. That's why it's so important to have liquid investments that can be accessed if inflation begins to increase. The Federal Reserve's inflation target is 2 to 3 percent growth per year, which is achieved by manipulating the monetary system.

The low inflation rate still means that the value of money in long-term investments, especially retirement money in 401(k)s, is losing 2 percent every single year—and that could add up big time. If you look at a 2 percent loss over a 30-year period, $10,000 today is only worth $4,000 30 years from now.

There are unintended consequences of the United States monetary policy.

CREDIT CARDS TO THE RESCUE

According to the Federal Reserve, credit card balances have topped $1 trillion.[41] And they keep growing.

According to Creditcards.com, the average APR on a credit card is at all-time highs, over 16 percent, despite benchmark interest rates at all-time lows.[42]

---

41   https://www.federalreserve.gov/releases/g19/current/g19.pdf

42   https://www.creditcards.com/credit-card-news/interest-rate-report-112117-unchanged-2121.php

So why do people rely so much on credit cards and lines of credit? Two primary reasons.

First, if you're saving or investing for retirement, that money is locked away in a pension, 401(k) or some other illiquid, tax-deferred vehicle. Even if you want to use the money, you don't, because it's earmarked for your long-term retirement strategy. You don't have excess savings for things like a car, college tuition, vacation, house repair, or deductibles on your automobile or homeowner's or medical insurance because it is likely in your retirement account. Because your money is in long-term instruments that can't necessarily be liquidated, you have to borrow from the bank instead for big expenses like a new car or major home repair.

The second reason people use credit is because they're just not good managers of their money. They spend more than they're bringing in, which forces them to supplement their earned income with credit.

THE PROBLEMS WITH BANK FINANCING

"Banking is very good business if you don't do anything dumb."
—WARREN BUFFETT

Learning about banking can prevent financial ruin and even make you wealthy. Most people are not educated about the proper use of loans and end up *being dumb*. Let's go through basic concepts so you can use banks to your advantage and prevent the common hardships they cause.

WHAT DO BANKS DO?

The role of banks has evolved over the years. They were once an institution that held personal savings and paid its customers a decent return on it. Today, savings account yields are measly, and most checking accounts now charge a servicing fee.

Banks are no longer an attractive institution to save money.

"A bank is a place where they lend you an umbrella in fair weather and ask for it back when it begins to rain."

—ROBERT FROST

The focus of banks is now lending, not paying interest on savings. The shift in priorities has caused customers to take risks to get a return on savings. The common way is investing it in the stock market, which you have learned is not a place for savings.

You will learn more about one of the best ways to store your savings in Chapter Seven.

Banks are great for facilitating transactions, such as

paying bills or receiving a paycheck. Their primary revenue source is lending. If you are educated about how to optimally use banks to your advantage, you too can win at their game. Here are the common loans you are likely to face in the future and how to approach them from a new perspective.

YOUR MORTGAGE

A home is the biggest purchase the average person makes. According to a study done by NerdWallet,[43] almost half of homebuyers would do something different if they were to buy again. The dissatisfaction is largely due to the complexity of the mortgage they choose, which is a function of trusting that the banker has your best interest in mind. Let's analyze the concept of a mortgage.

The typical financial advice to buy a home is as follows:

- Make the largest down payment possible.
- If you can afford it, bite the bullet with a 15-year (or lower) mortgage.
- If you take out a 30-year mortgage, pay it off as soon as possible with extra payments.

The conventional mindset of money hasn't worked up to this point of the book, and I am sorry to say the same

---

43   https://www.nerdwallet.com/blog/mortgages/2017-home-buyer-reality-report/

is true here: that mindset won't work when it comes to your mortgage, either.

Similar to how the 401(k) benefits Wall Street more than you, the common mortgage advice benefits the bank more than it does you. Through the perspective of The Perpetual Wealth Strategy, here is how to look at the advice:

Making a large down payment. A down payment comes from another account. If you liquidate that account, you exchange it for home equity. When you measure the benefit of the account versus the equity, you have the information to make an informed decision.

Home equity has a zero percent rate of return. A home's value will fluctuate based on the market, not by how much equity there is. If a house is worth $100,000 and rises in value by 10 percent, you have $10,000 in additional equity. That increase in equity occurs with a mortgage or without one. Therefore, *if* the account that your down payment originated from was earning a tax-free 5 percent annual return, your opportunity cost would be compounded by that return year after year, which adds up.

A big down payment is beneficial to the bank because they have a lower risk of losing money. If you defaulted on your mortgage and there was equity, the bank would foreclose on you, sell the home, and keep the equity.

There is no cookie-cutter solution that is applicable to everyone when determining their down payment amount or mortgage type. My response is always, "What would the bank do?" The bank would make the least amount of down payment possible and keep their money moving and earning.

A 15-Year Mortgage vs. a 30-Year Mortgage. This decision in mortgage payback term is motivated by the same intention as above: get rid of your mortgage as soon as possible. Why would you do that?

A 30-year fixed mortgage is far superior to a 15-year mortgage, and here is why:

- *Lower payment.* If you can afford a 15-year mortgage payment, get a 30-year and save the difference in an account that is earning interest.
- *Interest deduction.* For most people, the interest deduction on your mortgage makes it less expensive than face value.
- *Inflation reduces your mortgage payment.* Inflation is the goal of the United States Monetary Policy and is certain to happen each year. If inflation is 3 percent every year, your earned income will rise by that amount. Your mortgage payment will stay the same during this period, and because all other prices are going up, it gets cheaper every year.

For a mathematical breakdown of a 15-year versus a 30-year mortgage, I recorded a tutorial that is found in *The Financial Strategy Study Guide.*

The key to what lending advice is best for you is to look at the world through Wall Street or the bank's lens. What they provide us as advice always benefits them. A 15-year or lower term mortgage is what they want us to use when buying a house—that is why the interest rate is always less than a 30-year fixed loan. My question again is, "Why?"

It is an incentive for you, but it ultimately benefits them. A 15-year mortgage gives the bank less interest but higher cash flow—almost 30 percent higher. The bank can then use that cash flow to make more loans. A 15-year mortgage also creates more equity, benefiting the bank even more, with more collateral to secure their investment.

Do what the banks do, not what they tell you to do. If you have the necessary down payment, keep that in a vehicle that will earn interest. If you have the income to make a 15-year mortgage payment, save it and earn interest. This is what the banks do.

AUTOMOBILE LOANS

I have witnessed more bad decisions about buying a car than any other major financial decision. A few years ago,

I wrote an e-book that outlines how to choose the best automobile financing and how to get a good deal on every car you buy. There is a calculator included in *The Financial Strategy Study Guide* that teaches you how to analyze your options.

Here are the highlights:

- There is no such thing as a zero-percent loan. If that were true, a bank would not make any money. Typically, you give up a rebate in exchange for an incentive loan, which means you pay zero interest on a loan for a more expensive car than retail.
- Leasing versus financing depends on the car in question. Learning how to analyze the difference between a cash purchase, dealer financing, outside financing, or lease helps you buy better.
- Buying a car with cash comes with an opportunity cost because you withdrew the money from another account that could have earned you interest.

STUDENT LOANS

All loans are tools and neither good or bad inherently. The use of loans is what gets people into trouble and what has caused the student loan crisis at hand. The frightening statistics show a lack of understanding about simple financial principles—namely, the return on investment of a college education and the future obligation of paying the loan back:

- The outstanding student loan balance is over $1.4 trillion.
- Seventy percent of college students (45 million) have at least one student loan.[44]
- The average debt per borrower is $28,000.[45]
- Over the last 20 years, private college annual tuition has risen 130 percent, and public college tuition 212 percent.[46]
- In 1990, student loan balances were less than 29 percent of a graduate's total annual wages. Today, they are over 75 percent.[47]

I have worked with many families over the years who have either paid or planned to pay for their children's education. The sacrifice is commendable, but the method does not solve the issue.

If a family uses their savings to pay for college tuition and expenses, they give up what that money would have grown to and the cash flow it would have provided later in life.

44   https://studentloans.net/debt-per-graduate-statistics-2017

45   https://studentloans.net/debt-per-graduate-statistics-2017

46   https://www.cnbc.com/2017/11/29/how-much-college-tuition-has-increased-from-1988-to-2018.html

47   https://www.huffingtonpost.com/entry/3-charts-student-debt-crisis_us_56b0e9d0e4b0a1b96203d369

When mom and dad are older and cash flow is insufficient for their needs, the children are then burdened with the obligation to care for them.

The Financial Strategy Study Guide includes a video series that explains the math behind the dilemma and several options of what the family can do to recognize the issue at hand and make a decision that doesn't have unintended consequences.

Fundamentally, education in all forms is the transference of information that enhances a person's knowledge. In a professional context, successful education makes you more valuable to others. The result of a profitable education is that your earned income is proportionally higher than the cost.

In our day and age, tuition and student loan balances keep rising; however, wages and pay for college graduates remains stagnant.

Loans—such as a mortgage, automobile financing, a credit cards, or for educational purposes—aren't the problem. The grave statistics stated in this book reflect the uneducated use of these financial tools.

In the following chapters, you will learn how to look at financial life differently. This new perspective will positively influence your decisions and subsequently the results you are getting in your profession, earned income, cash flow, investments, and overall sense of financial freedom. The paradigm shift you are about to experience is paramount to capitalizing on the opportunities at hand, which include the use of specific financial tools that replace the need for Wall Street and banks.

KEY TAKEAWAYS

- Ask yourself these questions:
  - Are you saving or investing?
  - If you're investing, where are you investing, and what types of risks are you taking? How much control do you have?
  - Redefine what you consider an investment. Does an investment have to be a bond or a mutual fund or a stock?
- Typical investments (mutual funds, bonds, the stock market, 401(k)s, IRAs) are all priced based on speculation and manipulation of markets, interest rates, government backing, and ratings of the actual underlying investment. Are you subject to the unintended consequences of a manipulated market? Namely, inflation and the offset of any gains by the interest you are paying on loans.
- Breaking away from the typical mindset and services

of both Wall Street and banking is key to building your wealth and beginning the path to financial freedom.

CHAPTER 6

THINK FOR YOURSELF

"Rarely do we find men who willingly engage in hard, solid thinking. There is an almost universal quest for easy answers and half-baked solutions. Nothing pains some people more than having to think."

—MARTIN LUTHER KING, JR.

The experiences and circumstances of life, up to this very moment, have influenced the way we think. The way we think is the predominant force behind how we act. Our actions lead to our present-day results.

If you are not completely satisfied with your results and desire a better future, you must start by changing your thinking.

The thinking patterns that produce our words, statements,

and questions were impressed on us by our parents, community, friends, and professional environment. Equally influential were conduits like social media, TV, magazines, blogs, and books.

"You will be the same person in five years as you are today except for the people you meet and the books you read."

—CHARLIE JONES

Volitional change of your environment is the starting line. Surround yourself with people that inspire you, who encourage you, who push you to be better. Fill your mind with written and audible material that has the same impact. I promise you will see the results.

An example of a profound personal transformation that results from a shift in environment is my wife.

Synthia's upbringing was atypical of the American standard. Her neighborhood is in a relatively dangerous area of Hermosillo, Sonora—located in northwestern Mexico. She grew up in a simple cinderblock home with concrete floors and a metal roof. Her family never had a car. They vacationed only a few times to a small beach town 45 minutes away. She never had her own bed, and food was often scarce. She only had a few birthday parties growing up, and Christmas paled in comparison to what I was accustomed to.

You can hear her story firsthand, including her thoughts on mindset and environment, in an interview I did with her on *The Wealth Standard* podcast shortly after we arrived home from a humanitarian trip with a nonprofit organization called Stewfano (stewfano.org), which serves under-privileged children in Mexico.[48]

When we were married, Synthia's environment completely changed. She had to acclimate to a foreign country, culture, and language. The first few years were strenuous on both of us, and she faced a lot of pressure. However, her transformation is beyond impressive, and the lens she sees the world through today contrasts with what normally perpetuates in an upbringing like hers.

Humankind is designed to grow, improve, and constantly strive for better results.

Our past experiences, whatever they may be, influence our perception of the world, how we make decisions, and how we subsequently get results.

But they don't define our future.

If you want different results financially, the way you look at finances must change. That change can take place today. Books are a common catalyst to a paradigm shift and were

---

48 https://thewealthstandard.com/346422-2/

the medium for my own. The book that shaped my future has had a similar impact on others. It has sold more than 27 million copies and been translated into over 50 languages.

A LIFE-CHANGING BOOK

After going to college for a few years, mainly to play hockey, I decided to serve a mission for my church. Upon returning home to Connecticut, I decided to move west and finish up school at the University of Utah. I had about five months until the day of departure, so I decided to work. Through a temp agency, I found a position as the executive assistant to the director of the Hartford public school system's bilingual department. I had learned Spanish during my church service and wanted to keep my practice up. The placement counselor warned me about the position, stating I would be the fifth temp in sixth months. The department director was a stern Argentinian woman, and based on previous reports, the position was grueling. I love a challenge, so I signed up. Although the job was difficult, it was an incredible five months. On my last day, the department threw me a going-away party and gave me $500. Additionally, several individuals in the department attended our wedding.

One month into the position, my childhood friend Brandon insisted I read a book by Robert T. Kiyosaki called *Rich Dad Poor Dad*. It changed my life. Not only did it help me get through those five months, but it changed the way I looked at everything. The advice was 100 percent the opposite of what I had been taught. The narrative that was seared into my mind was "go to school, get a good job, save for retirement, and avoid debt like the plague." Kiyosaki's counter-philosophy resonated with me, because his poor dad was a successful teacher like my dad. Kiyosaki said, "The rich don't work for money; money works for them. Own your own business. Your house is not an asset. Invest for cash flow, not a nest egg."

I experienced the "Poor Dad" mentality growing up and had a front row seat to it in the Hartford Public School System. I decided that this is NOT what I wanted. Later in my life, I was fortunate to learn directly from this great man's knowledge. I have been privileged to share the stage with Robert on a few occasions. He and his wife are keynote speakers for the virtual financial event I co-host, called the Cash Flow Wealth Summit.[49] Additionally, his advisors have become good friends. A few have become business partners, and a few have become my clients.

POOR DAD TO RICH DAD

Let's dig in deeper to the Rich Dad philosophy.

Robert Kiyosaki describes four different financial mind-

---

49 www.cashflowwealthsummit.com

sets in his second book *Rich Dad's Cashflow Quadrant: Rich Dad's Guide to Financial Freedom.* He describes the four ways a person can produce cash flow: as an employee, a self-employed worker/small business owner, a large business owner, and an investor. A mindset is associated with each quadrant.

CASH FLOW QUADRANT
4 WAYS TO PRODUCE INCOME
LINEAR INCOME VS. LEVERAGED & RESIDUAL INCOME

EMPLOYEE
You have a job
No leverage
The amount of active work determines income

TIME = $

BUSINESS OWNER
You own a system
Leverage
Income does not depend on active work

EMPLOYEES = $$$

SELF-EMPLOYED
You own a job
No leverage
The amount of active work determines income

TIME = $

INVESTOR
You own investments
Leverage
Income does not depend on active work

YOUR MONEY WORKS FOR YOU = $$$

- **The employee quadrant (E quadrant):** Someone who trades their time for someone else's money (active work).
- **Small business and self-employed (S quadrant):** Someone who owns their own job or small business. They still do active work to make money.
- **Business owner (B quadrant):** Someone who owns a business with over 500 employees. This person is not actively performing work to make money.
- **Investor (I quadrant):** Someone who invests in business.

People in the S quadrant have a very dynamic mindset. They believe they own a business, and they also believe they're an investor, but they're neither. In the S quadrant, you can get away with not having systems, but as a company grows into the B quadrant, the business will fall apart if systems aren't instituted.

Kiyosaki considers a true business owner (B quadrant) to be someone running a business with over 500 employees, because at that stage, you need systems, processes, metrics, and a culture/value system. You must have a vision of where you're going.

The Investor quadrant (I quadrant) is a mindset. Kiyosaki doesn't consider real estate or a small business an investment. Investing is the mindset behind the opportunity.

I know brilliant real estate investors and I know those who despise it because they think real estate bankrupted them, which is why a quote by Robert himself is relevant: "There are no bad investments, only bad investors." Good investors see the world differently. They don't see excuses, challenges, obstacles, or reasons for giving up; they seek out the opportunity in everything.

The metaphor I use often on *The Wealth Standard* podcast also comes from Kiyosaki himself. Kiyosaki explains that there are three sides to a coin: heads, tails, and the edge. Heads is your opinion, tails is someone else's opinion. The edge is what he calls "the differentiator." It's where all the opportunity exists. An investor sits on the edge, forgoes their own perspective, and looks at both perspectives to see what the differences are and what the opportunity is. To be an investor, you need to take yourself out of your ego, out of the old saying, "It ain't what you don't know that gets you into trouble. It's what you know for sure that just ain't so." Once you realize this, then you'll look at everything differently.

YOUR FINANCIAL STATEMENT

The primary reason Robert Kiyosaki wrote *Rich Dad Poor Dad* was to induce people to play his board game Cashflow 101. The game is a practical way to begin looking at money differently. One of the primary lessons of the game is learning to use a financial statement as a tool to measure your financial life.

The basic financial statement consists of two components: the income statement and the balance sheet.

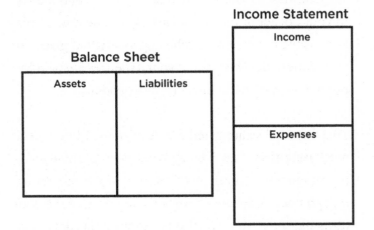

THE INCOME STATEMENT

This statement measures what comes in and what goes out every month. You can also look at it as what you are paid and what you pay others. If you have more coming in than going out, you are in positive cash flow. If you have more going out than coming in, you are in negative cash flow.

THE BALANCE SHEET

This statement measures what you own (assets) and what you owe (liabilities). You can also look at it as what you have that is of value and the value of what you are leasing/renting. If you have more assets than liabilities, you have a positive net worth or equity. If you owe others more than you own, you have negative equity or debt.

Kiyosaki makes the argument that a true asset puts money in your pocket or produces cash flow. The crux of his book is the concept of purchasing assets that give you cash flow, to the level where your expenses are paid for by your assets. That is financial independence.

This financial strategy led me down the path of solely purchasing assets that fit into this criterion. Over the years, my experience has been that these forms of assets—those that produce cash flow—benefit during the test of downturns and corrections and thrive during market upswings.

YOUR HUMAN CAPITAL STATEMENT

"If you want to be wealthy, make it your life's mission to continually create value for others."

—LES MCGUIRE

Several years ago, I was taught a perspective on the financial statement that truly changed my life. I have made a lot of money by understanding it.

A financial statement is simply a tool of measurement.

It is the measurement of human behavior—sp⟩
the behavior of whose statement it is. I call it th⟩
Capital Statement.

Earned income measures the value you have provided to someone else; the money is simply a receipt of that value. Expenses are the recognition of value in someone else, shown by your willingness to pay for it.

The assets that are producing the cash flow are your experience, talents, training, certifications—what others see as valuable enough to pay for. Liabilities are perhaps the things you're not good at or dislike doing but recognize that they are the assets of someone else.

The fact that someone pays you is proof that you are valuable. It's also proof that you can become *more* valuable, which requires investment in your human capital assets.

Magnification of these assets through training, certification, specialization, and experience will increase your value and subsequently increase your earned income.

"Try not to become a man of success, but rather try to become a man of value."

—ALBERT EINSTEIN

I often hear these words from others and in my own mind: "There isn't enough time."

If you've caught yourself saying this, it's a signal that your Human Capital Balance Sheet has too few liabilities. I have noticed in my life the insatiable desire to do everything myself so it's done the right way. It has cost me. Let me give you an example.

Many of us would argue that a lot of money could be saved each week by mowing the lawn and tending to the landscaping ourselves instead of hiring someone. I would argue that for most, it's a massive opportunity cost and an unproductive human capital asset that should be a liability.

If you make $100,000 per year and there are 2,080 work hours per year, that breaks down to an hourly wage of $48 per hour, your hourly value. If you cut the lawn yourself, the cost isn't just two hours a week. It's also the yearly maintenance, gasoline, cleanup, and lost time. If you pay the neighbor kid $20 to do the lawn or a professional company $50, you come out ahead if you replace those hours (even half of them) with productive value-creating activities that build assets that pay more than $48 per hour.

Establishing a healthy financial statement gets you out of the rat race. Establishing a healthy Human Capital Statement sets you on a path toward true financial freedom.

> *"The two most important days in your life are the day you are born and the day you find out why."*
>
> —MARK TWAIN

LeBron James is a great basketball player and it turns out he's savvy about business and understands the Human Capital Statement too. He's friends with Warren Buffet, Ray Dalio, Bill Gates, and many other successful moguls. He has leveraged his brand and name to meet with these business and investment icons, not to pick their brains about stock tips and investment ideas but to take the ideas he has and get their insight. Additionally, it's to learn to see as they see. James once said, "The first time I stepped on an NBA court, I became a businessman and a brand." Relationships, reputation, and your network are what I consider as the most valuable aspects of your Human Capital Statement. Leveraging the experience of others and the network of others is a powerful way to get on the fast track.

In 2009, *Sports Illustrated* did a study of former NFL and NBA players. The study showed that after only two years of retirement, 78 percent of NFL players were either broke or struggling financially. Within five years of retirement, 60 percent of NBA players were broke.

The average basketball career in the NBA lasts only 4.8 years. Because their earning window is limited by their physical well-being, a wise investment—not just in tangible assets but Human Capital Assets—is critical. Warren Buffet told LeBron to avoid get-rich-quick deals and to invest in business and what you know. James was an early investor in Beats before it was sold to Apple, and in the UK soccer team Liverpool F.C.—both incredibly successful ventures. Additionally, LeBron's activity in the virtual world has earned him a huge and loyal social media following. His name, brand, and value are clear. Even when his career is over, his influence will remain.

Many athletes fail to think of their short-term career as LeBron James did, as a business. The substantial amount of money a young athlete suddenly has is euphoric. It distracts the reality of the long-term consequences from assuming cash flow will last forever. They're living the high life without looking at the opportunities available to them to capitalize on the business environment that surrounds them. They don't understand or appreciate the value of publicity and exposure to the outside world, reputation, management, coaching, marketing, processes and organization, traditional and social media, endorsements and sponsorship, and a host of other aspects of the athletic entertainment world.

Hockey player Mario Lemieux went on to be one of the principal owners in the Pittsburgh Penguins. Former NBA star Charles Barkley became a primary endorser of Weight

Watchers and is a successful sports commentator. Baseball star Derek Jeter created a platform for pro athletes to talk directly to fans and started his own imprint at a publishing company.

Okay, you may not be a professional athlete like LeBron James or Mario Lemieux, but the principle equally applies to everyone.

You could argue that it's just as difficult for a second-generation wealthy person to maintain their wealth as it is for someone that's born in poverty to achieve wealth. It really comes down to three fundamental attributes: mindset, what people think they know, and what they're open to learning.

I love Carol Dweck's book *Mindset: The New Psychology of Success*. It talks about two different mindsets: a fixed mindset and a growth mindset. If you have a fixed mindset, you think your intelligence and talents are fixed traits—you have what you have and feel they're enough for success. You don't see much point in trying to improve on your skills because you think you already know everything you need to know. If you have a growth mindset, you have a lot more humility. You believe you always have more to learn and that your basic abilities can be developed and improved by working at them. You're open-minded and resilient, because you know you don't have all the answers.

BE YOUR BEST FINANCIAL ASSET

Robert Kiyosaki identifies an asset as something that puts money in your pocket. If you have employment where someone pays you, that is proof that you are an asset. If you are making more now than 10 years ago, that is proof that you can become a more valuable asset, and that process can continue infinitely.

I'm agnostic about what a person does for a career. Do what motivates you or what you're passionate about. Whatever that is, maximize your performance to be of the most value to someone else. Invest in yourself, the greatest asset of all. Take online classes, get certified, look for opportunities. Think of yourself as your main financial asset before you look at anything external to make you more money. Realize that the responsibility is on your shoulders—not the circumstances of the economy, not the market, or interest rates, or some outside factor.

Take responsibility for who you are and what you do. Invest in yourself before you invest in anything else. Understand who you are, what your strengths and core competencies are, what you want from life. Beyond just understanding yourself, strive to maximize your understanding of leadership, organization, markets, how to create a team, and how to bring on partners.

You don't have to get hung up on degrees. Most people associate accreditations with success, but it's not that straightforward. An MBA will get you an interview, but an MBA won't get you a meaningful profession. And does an MBA make a person wealthy? I know bankrupt people with MBAs and PhDs, and I know super-wealthy people that have no college education at all.

Does education have to be formal? I would say (especially these days), a resounding *no*. We have access to more knowledge with the press of a button than could be consumed in a lifetime. The utilization of information is the secret, and that can only be done practically through experience. Informal education and experience can teach you so much more than a business school can.

Your relationships are an asset just the way a piece of property or a business are. Wealthy and successful people view relationships not as competition but as assets. Investing in your core relationships is one of the most profound investments ever. I associate everything I've ever done with a relationship.

The key to the growth of your relationship assets is the investment you make that starts with the motivation of seeking to create value for them. Introduce them to people they'd find interesting. Send them articles you think they'd like to read.

early on that the platitude of "Can I do anything ?" is apathetic. The proactive pursuit of influencing one's life for the better, figuring out their challenge or opportunity, and providing insight appropriately, is magic. The Law of Compensation conceptualized by the great American philosopher Ralph Waldo Emerson teaches that there is a dualism in everyone's life. There are elements that are working and elements that are not. If you are the helpmate and shore up deficiency, remuneration is lawfully yours.

If you feel a connection with someone, chances are they feel the same connection with you. If they have an awesome experience with you, you're going to be top of mind when they talk to others. If there's a situation that's relevant to your interests, they're going to think of you and say, "Oh, you should talk to this guy."

Investment in yourself gives you the highest returns with the least amount of risk ensuring that you will always win and never lose. The mindset of you becoming your greatest asset inspires continual introspection, taking inventory of how you create value for others and the pursuit of opportunities to keep learning and growing.

HOW DO THE WEALTHY THINK DIFFERENTLY?

"The rich don't do things differently than the poor, they do the exact opposite."

—ROBERT KIYOSAKI

LeBron James and the others nailed it by looking at the world not through the eyes of a celebrity but as businessmen. They recognized that outside of themselves, they are a brand, an image, and a celebrity. They leveraged the experience and the expertise of others to enhance their Human Capital Assets. First, by building a network of those who had proven themselves in business and investment, not the talking-head financial celebrities. Second, by paying attention to the industry they were in and the multiple ways it offered them post-career opportunities.

The wealthy have other unique characteristics. Here are a few examples of what the rich do:

· They value people and ideas, not things.
· They seek opportunities to serve and create value for others, and do not take advantage or exploit others.
· They rise to the challenge of any circumstance and become the hero rather than the victim.
· They are mission- and purpose-driven, not results-driven.
· Their best investment is never outside of themselves.

It's inside themselves through personal development and businesses that they influence and control.

- They take risks they can control.
- They have a growth mindset, not a fixed mindset.
- They use money to help people, not people to make money.

Society is conditioned to look at life as dog-eat-dog, which means the only way to be successful is by winning at the expense of another's loss, often referred to as a zero-sum game.

The mantra of the wealthy is *win-win or no deal*. They realize that relationships, reputation, and improving the lives of other people are going to subsequently improve their own lives.

A quote from Adam Smith, the social philosopher and economist who was a key figure in the Scottish Enlightenment of the 18th century, magnifies the idea.

He wrote,

> [The rich] consume little more than the poor, and in spite of their natural selfishness and rapacity...they divide with the poor the produce of all their improvements. They are led by an invisible hand to make nearly the same distribution of the necessaries of life,

which would have been made, had the earth been divided into equal portions among all its inhabitants, and thus without intending it, without knowing it, advance the interest of the society, and afford means to the multiplication of the species.[50]

What Smith means is that the wealthy are compelled to gain, as are all of us. However, it is a non-zero-sum gain. In the process, their innovation, risk tolerance, and intention ultimately improve the lives of all.

The wealthy have a growth mindset. Failure doesn't exist, only lessons. They are always learning and never arrive. They don't take criticism as a personal attack; they take criticism as an opportunity to get feedback from another perspective and grow.

If you want to be in a better place financially, start with yourself and determine if you have a fixed or a growth mindset. Then, identify your Human Capital Assets and seek to build more of them through relationships, education, and shifting from the intention to get to the intention to give.

Finally, associate with like-minded individuals. Turn your Facebook or social media experience into a virtual

---

50 https://www.adamsmith.org/adam-smith-quotes/

mastermind group.[51] Avoid friends that don't influence you for good, and follow those that inspire you to be better and do more. Jim Rohn said, "You are the average of the five people you surround yourself with."

FINDING LIKE-MINDED PEOPLE

For individuals and entrepreneurs:

- Meetup.com
- Groupspaces.com
- Meetin.org
- Coworker.org
- Co-working spaces such as WeWork (https://www.wework.com/)

For small to medium business owners:

- Vistage (https://www.vistage.com/)
- Entrepreneurs' Organization (EO) (https://www.eonetwork.org/)
- YPO (https://www.ypo.org/)
- Founders Society (https://foundersnetwork.com/)
- YEC (https://yec.co/)
- Strategic Coach (www.strategiccoach.com)

---

51 https://en.wikipedia.org/wiki/Mastermind_group

An example of how influential your environment is can be found in a book called *Family Fortunes: How to Build Family Wealth and Hold on to It for 100 Years*, by Bill Bonner.

HAITI VS. SWITZERLAND

Haiti is one of the poorest countries in the world, and Switzerland is one of the richest. Switzerland has few natural resources and extremely harsh, cold winters; Haiti has an abundance of resources, fertile soil, and beautiful weather year-round.

How is Switzerland so wealthy and Haiti so poor?

A hundred years ago, if you lived in Switzerland, to survive the winters, preparation and discipline were paramount. Innovative and disciplined farming was a necessity; so was the efficient storage and consumption of food. Equitable trade was also air-tight due to the potential consequences during winter months. If you failed to prepare, you did not survive. That mentality perpetuated to the next generation and then to the next. Today, the winter months are still harsh, but with modern technology, it is much easier to survive. The ingrained discipline, however, remains. It has influenced business, foreign relations, and trade, and has made Switzerland one of the wealthiest nations in the world.

A hundred years ago, if you lived in Haiti, survival was

simple. The environment was rich with resources. The soil was such that if you planted anything it would grow, year-round. The weather was rarely harsh and didn't threaten life. However, the abundance created a different mentality. The discipline to be efficient and prepare didn't exist, as life wasn't on the line. Today, it is evident that although Haiti still has an abundance of resources, the discipline and mindset to be resourceful doesn't exist.

Society has conditioned the belief that individual effort is the ideal and group effort is cheating. The power of identifying everyone's talent and skillset within the framework of a team or group, and then dividing the corresponding roles and responsibilities, is one of the most profound forces in business and one of the catalysts to wealth.

EMBRACING YOUR NEW MINDSET

The quickest way to more money is to maximize your earned income. You maximize income by creating more value for others. Your Human Capital Statement will give you clues to discover exactly how.

A traditional financial health assessment shows the state of your finances. Typically, financial advisors will look for opportunities here to help you increase your wealth. There are strategies to reduce your taxes, increase the rate of return of your investments, and reduce high-interest debt. Most financial advice will be similar here, no matter the firm that the advisor represents.

However, the results of improving the financial statement alone pale in comparison to maximizing your Human Capital Statement.

The assessment of your Human Capital Statement—namely, those assets that are currently producing your income and the liabilities that are taking some of it—show your biggest opportunity. Focus on enhancing or adding to your human capital assets, especially those activities that inspire and give you energy. Then, delegate your liabilities to those people who consider them assets. These relationships in your network will do a much better job and save you not only money but time, patience, and energy.

Examples of these assets include:

- Your core competencies, talents, and strengths
- Your professional training, experience, and credentials
- Your key relationships
- Your key business contacts
- Your key business opportunities
- Your reputation

Most people don't know what their assets are, let alone those of others. I recommend investing in one of the many rsonal assessment tests that help you evaluate your strengths, what you gravitate toward, and what you are resistant to. The most widely used are the Myers-Briggs Type Indicator test,[52] DiSC personal assessment tool,[53] Gallup's Strengths Finder,[54] and the Kolbe A Index.[55]

Knowing more about you can help you in myriad ways. For example, if you don't know how you prefer to integrate in a team, you could be like a bull in a china shop. You could mess everything up because you don't understand what role you play based on your natural competencies or abilities.

Personal assessments don't tell you you're good or bad; they just define your tendencies, strengths, genius, and unique abilities, and subsequently where you should focus your time. Let's say one of these assessments shows I have a resistance in X area. That's not a judgment. It's just feedback. Well, now I know where I have resistance, which is very valuable information. I don't necessarily have to try to fix it. Instead, I now realize that when something in the X area comes up, I'm better off knowing someone whose unique genius (area of expertise) it is. At the same time, the tests can show where you shine

---

52 http://www.myersbriggs.org/my-mbti-personality-type/

53 https://www.discprofile.com/what-is-disc/overview/

54 https://www.gallupstrengthscenter.com/

55 http://m.kolbe.com/aindex

and point you in directions that will make the best use of your strengths.

THE EXAMPLE OF HENRY FORD

In the early 1900s, renowned entrepreneur Henry Ford was frequently mocked by the media for his ignorance and low level of intelligence—even as an enemy of the nation. Ford sued the *Chicago Tribune* for libel in 1916, and the case went to trial. Over the 14-week trial, Henry Ford spent eight days on the witness stand answering questions to prove his intelligence. During the lengthy engagement, Ford became frustrated and made the following profound statement:

> If I should really *want* to answer the foolish question you have just asked, or any of the other questions you have been asking me, let me remind you that I have a row of electric push-buttons on my desk, and by pushing the right button, I can summon to my aid men who can answer *any* question I desire to ask concerning the business to which I am devoting most of my efforts. Now, will you kindly tell me, *why* I should clutter up my mind with general knowledge, for the purpose of being able to answer questions, when I have men around me who can supply any knowledge I require?[56]

---

56 Napoleon Hill, *Think and Grow Rich*, Chapter 5.

Iconic men and woman are often categorized as an omniscient archetype in our minds. I argue that iconic men and women of past times and today discovered their genius and surrounded themselves with those who have discovered theirs.

A client of mine owns franchises in the oil change business. He's successful because he learned how to operate a system. One day while we were talking, he said, "I'm thinking of selling a percentage of the franchises and investing it. I have a potential buyer who is offering to buy 40 percent. What should I do with that money? Should I put it into cashflowing properties and apartments or somewhere else?"

He was in his early forties at the time, and he lived in southern California. I said, "You're young, and you could put that money into apartments, but then what are you going to do? Are you just going to sit around the beach and hang out with your kids all day?"

I said, "*You* are the asset here. Look at the skillset you've acquired over the last decade. Could you replicate that in another industry?" He eventually made some real estate investments, but he also explored other franchise opportunities where the business model already existed and just needed a good operator to implement it. He found partners, and they've opened some healthy fast food franchises, with more in the works.

He had an awesome business that was bought out because it was so successful. He invested back into a franchise operation in a different field because he already knew he was an expert at it. He wanted to do it again with something else. That was his core competency. As an asset, it's one of the rarest out there. Operating a business and having the corresponding leadership characteristics are some of the most valuable skills in the market today—more than any tangible thing.

I would call him a serial entrepreneur. He discovered, as all serial entrepreneurs do, that he was good at building a business but not that interested in running it once it becomes established. Although he went on to build a new franchise chain, just in a different sort of market, the type of business wasn't that important. For successful entrepreneurs, it's resource vs. resourcefulness. That's agnostic to the actual business.

For a lot of serial entrepreneurs, the excitement of opening a new business is addictive. When the novelty wears off and the business is running smoothly, everything becomes routine and they get bored. They're no longer engaged, and their thoughts turn to the next opportunity. Ultimately, this ongoing pursuit lacks luster until a greater purpose beyond success is discovered.

> *"People claim to want to do something that matters, yet they measure themselves against things that don't, and track their progress not in years but in microseconds. They want to make something timeless, but they focus instead on immediate payoffs and instant gratification."*
>
> —RYAN HOLIDAY, *PERENNIAL SELLER: THE ART OF MAKING AND MARKETING WORK THAT LASTS*

If you look at the core foundation of any long-term fulfilling business, it is purpose driven. What is our purpose? What are we doing? What's our mission? Why are we doing this? If your purpose isn't clear, or if there isn't a deep-seeded passion behind it, then you and your business won't thrive *perennially*.

THE NEXT STEP: BUILD YOUR HUMAN CAPITAL STATEMENT

"What lies behind us and what lies before us are tiny matters compared to what lies within us."

—RALPH WALDO EMERSON

No physical asset can compare to the greatest asset of all: you. You are the source of all wealth you have created and will create. Your capacity to do so is infinite. To experience true financial freedom, a healthy income statement is simply one part. The other, and most important, is to discover how to give the greatest value within you to the greatest number of people. Knowing your options comes down to knowing who you are as an asset and then figuring out what you want. Once you know that, you can assess opportunities and decide which options will help you get from where you are right now and where you want to be.

What are your assets? Identify your strengths, core competencies, and passions.

What are your liabilities? List them.

What are you paid for, and how well does it align with your assets?

What do you pay for, and how well does it align with your liabilities?

As you work to align your earned income with your true assets, it will go up. Part of the process might entail the identification of liabilities such as being a handyman, mowing the lawn, doing your taxes, or washing your car. Your expenses will go up, but the time it frees lets you leverage your assets.

This understanding is why most wealthy people don't just hang it up at 65 and go play golf for the rest of their life. They've found something that is purposeful and meaningful, and that they're so passionate about they don't even consider it work—it's their calling. They don't feel burdened by 12-hour days and six- or even seven-day work weeks, because they're doing something they love and are driven by the desire to be more and do more.

If you're achieving work you love, it's a milestone along the journey. What is it going to take to get to that milestone? What are the opportunities, and what's a good first step?

We're all wired to want the sense of accomplishment and fulfillment that comes from building something worthwhile. Figure out what drives you and put it to use. If you don't like what you're doing for your work—stop doing it. Chances are, if you don't like what you're doing by now, you're never going to like it. Use assessment tools to figure out what you do want, what you're passionate about, and then find a way to use that passion in your career.

Now that we have mindset straight, let's talk about how to take resourcefulness and apply it to specific tools. A tool or resource will never make you rich, but the use of it will. Look at golf. Lots of golfers spend money on their clubs as something that will improve their game, as opposed to improving themselves, which will ultimately improve their game. Pro golfers could play with a set of cheap secondhand clubs and still beat you. In the end, it's not expensive, high-status clubs that win. Winning = mindset + experience + tools.

KEY TAKEAWAYS

- Your financial results are a function of what you do. What you do is a function of who you are. Who you are is a function of how you think.
- Learn to think like the wealthy by reading, studying, and surrounding yourself with like-minded people.
- Your Human Capital Statement organizes, focuses, and guides you to optimize your financial life.

You have learned so far that financial success starts with your mindset, which influences the way you use financial tools. In the next chapter, you will learn more about a financial tool that serves as the foundation for the wealthy, banks, and corporations.

CHAPTER 7

A SOLID FOUNDATION

"Everyone has the ability to build a financial ark to survive and flourish in the future. But you must invest time in your financial education to build an ark with a solid foundation."

—ROBERT KIYOSAKI

Your financial statement is the scorecard that measures wealth-building activities—saving and investing. Your Human Capital Statement helps you identify wealth-creating opportunities—making more money.

My experience with many business owners and investors has taught me that wealth building has a foundation upon which your assets and liabilities grow. It's not your entire financial strategy—but it's arguably the most vital. The financial tool we recommend as your foundation dates to the turn of the twentieth century and has been used by wealthy families, big banks, and corporations. These guys understand the value of liquidity—they are the ones who capitalize on market downturns. This understanding originates from decades of experience with market and business cycles and the knowledge that life doesn't always work out as planned. They are prepared to prosper in those moments because they have a solid foundation.

I met Martin in 2011. He was a real estate developer, author, and entrepreneur—having started several businesses. He seemed to be wealthy—had a big house, drove a fancy SUV, and traveled to exotic places. Martin was charismatic. We had similar philosophical interests and hit it off immediately. I told him about my business and my perspective on securing a financial foundation before investing. Although my specialization intrigued him—setting up what I call The Wealth Maximization Account™—he sneered at me, sat back in his chair and, shaking his head, said, "Savings is for losers. I can make a 30 percent return in my sleep—that's a hard sell to a guy like me, Pat."

Years earlier, before 2008, I heard this statement a lot. Martin's words seemed to replay in my mind in slow motion, bringing back some not-so-fond memories of my personal liquidity crisis and those of many people I knew. I must admit, Martin's words caught me a little off guard since the aftermath of the crisis was still palpable.

Years later, Martin connected with me through a text—apparently one of his businesses had lost its biggest contract and his tech start-up was running out of cash. He only had two months left. He needed a $75,000 loan. His situation escalated from there and he was forced to take on partners and give them a hefty percentage of the companies. Martin had made millions, probably tens of millions up to that point, but he couldn't come up with $75,000. Fortunately, his business did rebound, but his share of the company was less now—much less.

Martin would have benefited from a solid foundation.

YOUR FOUNDATION: THE WEALTH MAXIMIZATION ACCOUNT

Imagine what you would want out of a foundational asset before you started to put a portion of your assets and earned income into it. What would you want the account benefits to be? Here are the common responses I have received over the years:

- Availability or liquidity on demand
- A good return
- Insured or guaranteed to not lose money
- Tax favorability
- A simple transfer of ownership
- Private and possibly protected from creditors

o limit to yearly contribution amounts
- Offered and administered by a reputable company

The Wealth Maximization Account (WMA) offers you these attributes and more.

The WMA is a uniquely designed whole life insurance policy with a paid-up additions (PUA) rider that creates instant liquidity. It is offered by a private mutual insurance company.

The design of the policy, specifically how much PUA can be added, adheres to the Internal Revenue Code Section 7702, which defines the maximum contribution level of a life insurance policy without the growth being taxed.

A mutual life insurance company is a private corporation owned by specific account owners, referred to as participating policyholders. Participating also refers to the payment of company profits to policyowners through a dividend.

The WMA is your ideal foundational asset. It is the only asset that exists to offer numerous foundational benefits. The growth is free from income, dividend, or capital gains tax. The cash value is liquid. Annual growth is contractually guaranteed. If the insurance company is profitable, they distribute a dividend on a pro rata basis to each policyowner. The insurance company guarantees a line of credit against the total amount of policy cash value. The value is private and typically not subject to the claims of creditors. The face value or death benefit protects the beneficiaries against the policyholder's premature death. The death benefit can satisfy creditors, settle business or real estate debts, fund college education, pass on a legacy, and more. The policy can be pledged as collateral and can be used to improve the financial situation of an individual, investor, or business owner.

To be fair, the WMA isn't going to yield double digits per year. By itself, it isn't going to make you wealthy. Rather, it's your foundation, where you store your reserves. It also fulfills much of the benefit of a typical investment, such as a mutual fund. When you factor in the tax benefits and low costs, the typical market investment mutual fund has trouble outperforming the WMA after fees and taxes. I'll show you some examples in later chapters.

Will your insurance policy give you the returns you need to have all your dreams come true through the magic of compound interest and tax-free cash flow? Maybe, maybe not—that is why it is the foundation, not where *all* your wealth is stored.

The following is a simple way to categorize the WMA and other types of assets you may acquire to build your wealth.

CLASSIFYING ASSETS

"The individual investor should act consistently as an investor and not as a speculator."

—BEN GRAHAM

I like to classify assets in terms of risk and control and get the highest benefit for each class (rate of return). The more control you have over the asset, the less risk you have. The WMA is the ideal foundation because you have optimal control, protection, and a great return.

To classify other assets by these terms (risk and control), I developed an easy-to-understand model that helps you prioritize wealth building. I call it The Hierarchy of Wealth™, modeled after the famed psychological model, Maslow's Hierarchy of Needs.

The Hierarchy of Needs, developed by psychologist Abraham Maslow, is a five-stage model that describes the motivation behind human behavior and does so sequentially. The foundation is Physiological, then Safety, Belonging, Self-Esteem, and finally Self-Actualization.[57] Maslow found that you must have your physical needs like

---

57 Physiological needs: air, food, drink, shelter, warmth, sex, sleep. Safety needs: protection from elements, security, order, law, stability, freedom from fear. Belonging needs: friendship, intimacy, trust, acceptance, receiving and giving love, affiliating with a group. Self-esteem needs: esteem for oneself (dignity, achievement, mastery, independence), and the desire for reputation or respect from others. Self-actualization needs: realizing personal potential, self-fulfillment, seeking personal growth and peak experiences, and a desire to become what one is capable of.

food and shelter before you seek safety such as humane living conditions or a stable community. These needs come before the innate desire for relationships, and then your pursuit of self-esteem comes after that. Finally, discovering your purpose and passion—what Maslow calls self-actualization—comes last. With this model, you can't skip steps. You don't fulfil your physiological needs and go right to discovering your purpose. Needs are fulfilled sequentially—one step at a time.

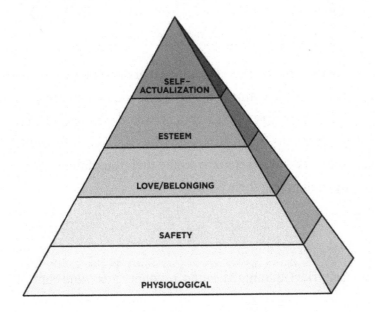

The Hierarchy of Needs model parallels the financial strategy I teach, The Hierarchy of Wealth. You start with the foundation—Tier 1, your safest capital—and build step by step through Tiers 2, 3, and then 4.

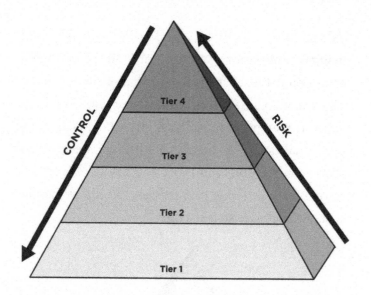

I work with clients to maximize their income-producing potential and optimize their financial statement. The goal is to put away 15 to 20 percent of earned income and then reallocate assets to align with The Hierarchy of Wealth. One of the first steps is to secure their foundation, Tier 1, by capitalizing their WMA.

Tier 1

Criteria: Guaranteed, liquid, prudent return, and control

Strategy: Put away 15-20 percent of earned income and establish 6–24 months of living expenses before moving to Tier 2.[58]

---

58   In *The Financial Strategy Study Guide,* I've made a video that illustrates the amount of money that leaves an average American's fingertips each month. It shows how you can more than double your wealth with a few simple adjustments. It is called the Maximum Potential Calculator.

Tier 2

Criteria: Control, collateral, cash flow, and consistency

Strategy: Invest in your personal development to make more money, which includes investing in your business. Invest in hard assets like residential real estate that you own, control, and that produces passive cash flow that you don't work for.

Tier 3

Criteria: No guarantees, limited collateral, no control, or control is relinquished to a professional.

Strategy: Once you have maximized your Tier 1 and Tier 2 assets, Tier 3 investments are next. They provide higher returns and have higher risk. Examples are hard money lending against collateral, or syndicated funds for hard assets such as real estate or commodities.

Tier 4

Criteria: No guarantees, no collateral, speculative, could lose 100 percent of the investment.

Strategy: Tier 4 is speculative investments where you can lose everything. This tier comes after at least 90 percent of your assets are in their respective Tiers 1, 2, and 3.

The Hierarchy of Wealth is a system that works. When used properly, it will make you wealthy. I have seen hundreds of different investments, strategies, and businesses. Some work. Many do not. Nobody sets out in business or investing with the intent of losing money; however, change happens—your wealth will always be subject to volatility, economic disruption, failed partnerships, new trends, technology, etc.

The bedrock of The Wealth Maximization Account provides you with the framework to conquer all these challenges and more.

Unfortunately, most individuals are simply hoping that Wall Street or a money manager will do all of this for them. Unfortunately, the typical financial strategy is built on a house of cards and, therefore, during market downturns 401(k)s become 201(k)s.

The approach most are taking with their wealth ends up looking like the opposite of The Hierarchy of Wealth—an inverted pyramid—where the riskiest assets have become their financial foundation and those assets that are the safest and most secure are at the top. When financial change comes like a recession or market downturn, those with an inverted pyramid are wiped out, and those with a solid foundation typically pick up the pieces, take advantage of opportunities, and do very well.

Adhering to The Hierarchy of Wealth ensures you are on top—*Heads You Win, Tails They Lose.*

THE VALUE OF LIQUIDITY DURING UNCERTAIN TIMES

I met Allan, a securities and tax attorney, during the spring of 2010. He had been clobbered by the real estate debacle and was unwinding several projects that had gone south. Fortunately, he landed an exclusive contract with another firm and investment group that paid him $200 per hour. He was working 70-hour weeks trying to dig himself out.

We hit it off immediately—we were both going through many of the same challenges. He taught me a ton about real estate and securities law. The amount of fraud he witnessed during the real estate boom scared us both; we were very cautious about who could be trusted.

Allan had hunkered down and was committed to settling his debts, shutting down his real estate projects, and socking money away. He immediately grasped the idea of The Wealth Maximization Account. He understood its asset protection characteristics, tax benefits, and of course, the fact that the guarantees prevent loss, even in a market decline. However, we met during a period of extreme adversity and uncertainty and he was reluctant to make a move.

The final decision was to replace his expensive term life policy with a convertible term policy, which was less expensive and gave him more coverage. The goal was to convert parts of it over time to multiple Wealth Maximization Accounts as his situation changed.

Allan took a long time to make the decision to start shifting his assets and savings. We met every year or so for three years, at which point he decided to convert enough for a $5,000 per year WMA. The size was extremely small relative to his earned income, but because I knew his cautious state of mind, I understood.

The year after, Allan had all his debts paid off and was in the clear regarding his real estate debacle. He had amassed savings of $200,000. He was six to 12 months away from beginning a real estate development project where he would be one of the principals. He would need to invest somewhere between $100,000 and $300,000 of his own capital in the project. He was comfortable saving $50,000 per year and could commit for seven years at this level. It took Allan several years to feel comfortable enough to go all-in with a WMA as his primary savings vehicle and primary source for his opportunity fund. He's financially better off—and he's emotionally better off as well. He considers his decision the best financial move he has ever made.

The hardest part of shifting your thinking is going against

the conventional wisdom of typical financial planning and advice—max out your 401(k) contributions, invest in mutual funds, and bet on the stock market for long-term returns and wealth. It's hard to buck the advice that just about every financial advisor gives you. It's hard to explain to your family and friends why you're doing something so different. You might also mistakenly think it's hard and complicated to set up these accounts and that you'll need to pay an advisor a ton of money to do it right. All those pressures might combine to keep you from acting in your own financial interest.

KEY TAKEAWAYS

- The wealthy think differently. They don't gamble and sacrifice their wealth.
- You are your own best financial asset. No other asset can replace an investment in yourself through training and education.
- Know yourself. Use personality assessments to learn your strengths and weaknesses and find the work you love.
- Know your options and leverage them.
- Use The Hierarchy of Wealth to position your current assets and prioritize new investments you make.

Now it's time to take what you've learned so far and apply it.

CHAPTER 8

BE LIKE THE WEALTHY

"It's simple arithmetic: Your income can grow only to the extent that you do."

—T. HARV EKER

One of our company values at Paradigm Life is BE-DO-HAVE, and I strive daily to live it. We instinctively want to grow and have more. Paradoxically, most of us carry the thought pattern, "Once I have [fill in the blank of whatever you want], then I will be [fill in the blank]." For example, you might think, "If I got that promotion, then I would be able to afford that house." Or maybe, "If my investment doubles, I will have more freedom."

Having is a function of doing. The reason you don't have something is because you haven't become the person who creates sufficient value to justify what you might get in return.

, the counsel is three simple steps:

k out the person who has the results you desire.
2. ᴅᵢscover what they are doing differently, then distinguish their behavior compared to yours (work ethic, interaction with others, schedule, organization, etc.).
3. Adopt their behavior, mimic their interactions—embody who they are.

When it comes to wealth, the formula isn't any different.

Be: If you want the results of wealth, you must acknowledge that who you are hasn't sufficiently developed into the person who produces that measurement of value. Therefore, focus on yourself and the tremendous opportunity to course correct and be that person who warrants wealth. Study the person who *already* has what you're seeking: their persona, their characteristics, their demeanor, and overall behavior.

Do: Your behavior will change. The way you interact with others, your vocabulary, your schedule, your work ethic, will be different.

Have: Money is simply the exchange of value. Those who have the money exchange it for what they value more than money. As you evolve into a wealthy being, you will naturally be driven to create more value for others. That value is reciprocated with money.

HOW THE WEALTHY *USE* INSURANCE TO GROW THEIR WEALTH

Observe families that have been around for a long time and have passed wealth from generation to generation. Their objective isn't just obtaining present-day wealth; it's also perpetuating that wealth into the future for their heirs.

One of the best parts of what I do is meeting amazing people. On my podcast, *The Wealth Standard,* I interviewed David Drake, a family member of a family office in New York City. (Family offices serve very wealthy families by providing traditional private wealth management along with handling nonfinancial issues, such as private schooling, travel arrangements, and other household arrangements. Some family offices build their business by serving many clients.)[59]

It was a fascinating conversation. We spent much of the interview discussing the significant focus family offices place on training and educating family members. It was crystal clear that they fully understood the BE-DO-HAVE principle.

The Rockefeller family is a perfect example of BE-DO-HAVE as it relates to wealth—not just creating it, but preserving it. John D. Rockefeller made his fortune in oil. When he died, he had amassed a fortune of more than $1.5

---

59 https://www.investopedia.com/terms/f/family-offices.asp

billion. During that same era, another iconic figure, Cornelius Vanderbilt, amassed a fortune of over $100 million, the equivalent of over $215 billion in today's dollars. The difference is that today, the Rockefeller fortune continues to grow. The Vanderbilt fortune is completely gone.

What distinguishes the two families? The Rockefellers hold to a set of values, known as the Rockefeller Rules, similar to the BE-DO-HAVE idea. Through dynamic estate planning and wealth management, their family office not only manages and perpetuates wealth, but it also ensures that the heirs are taught and educated accordingly.

The Vanderbilt legacy did not align with the mindset that created the fortune in the first place. They had wealth yet were not wealthy. Although Cornelius Vanderbilt himself understood wealth, he never had the education and mindset to create a strategic plan that would ensure that his heirs would hold to the same standards. In 1973, Vanderbilt University held a family reunion. Over 100 direct heirs attended the reunion, and not one was a millionaire.[60]

How do the Rockefellers and other dynasty families manage their wealth across the generations?

They place significant focus on the heirs' personal devel-

---

60 https://www.forbes.com/sites/natalierobehmed/2014/07/14/
      the-vanderbilts-how-american-royalty-lost-their-crown-jewels/#c2c3354353ba

opment. They also diversify their investments, including real estate and business holdings, natural resources, and equities.

One of the most common foundational strategies is holding a permanent cash value insurance policy on every heir, with a mutual insurance company.

The Kennedy family, another dynasty with extensive real estate holdings and business interests, uses this tactic going back to the patriarch Joe Kennedy in the 1920s.

These wealthy families, and many others like them, stored and continue to store most of their foundational wealth in financial products that are guaranteed, not volatile, and that provide a range of benefits.

Today, the achievement of a wealthy mindset conflicts with what most Americans are becoming. The attitude of go to school, get a job with good benefits, and save money in the stock market through your 401(k) is breeding mediocrity. It's a complete contradiction to what wealthy people have done. We ask ourselves: Why is the country in such bad shape? Why is there so much credit card debt? Why is there so much student loan debt? Why are people living paycheck to paycheck?

Go back and look at that BE-DO-HAVE principle. It says

it doesn't matter who you are. Executives, famous people, dynasty families are doing the opposite of the typical American. Their greatest assets are people, relationships, and personal development—themselves. Their financial strategy is based on certainty, not rolling the dice.

INSURANCE-BASED FINANCIAL STRATEGIES

Banks and corporations hold billions of dollars in an asset that most Americans have never heard of, let alone own themselves: cash value life insurance.[61]

Life insurance in America started in the mid-1700s in social institutions such as churches, charitable and fraternal organizations, and small communities. Many of the major mutual life insurance companies—Penn Mutual, New York Life, Mass Mutual, and others—started when people in these groups pooled money that would be paid out in the event a member of the group died. These groups were formed for mutual support, not to make a profit. They didn't have shareholders or boards. They were mutual insurance companies owned by the policyholders.

Back then, life insurance through a mutual company served a moral function—managing a pool of money for the benefit of those left behind after a breadwinner died.

---

61 https://www.gao.gov/assets/250/242259.html; https://www.bankdirector.com/committees/compensation/boli-market-remain-steady-2018

Life insurance policies today serve the same function, just through much bigger institutions, with more sophisticated investment strategies. If the mutual company makes a profit, it's distributed to the policyholders.

When insurance started, it was vanilla. In the beginning, a policy was permanent—it was active for the whole life of the insured person. (Term life insurance, which covered the insured person only for a specified time, came later.) If the policyholder stopped paying into the pool, they'd lose all the benefits, and they'd lose the money they put in.

Life insurance started becoming more sophisticated as time went by. By the late 1800s, policies were still permanent, but they accumulated a refund value, also known as a cash surrender value. This means that if you put money into a policy, but at some point couldn't keep paying or canceled the policy, you didn't walk away with nothing; you'd get a cash payment based on how much you paid in.

FARMER SAVINGS ACCOUNT

When insurance started to become an industry in the 1800s, most people were farmers. They might have had some money in the bank, but that money didn't earn interest. Banks in those days were largely unregulated, and the risk of a failure was very real. Insurance was a much better, much safer savings vehicle. It paid interest and was a more secure way to pass on any accumulated wealth.

Back then, farmers didn't get subsidized like they are today—they didn't have a consistent income and cash flow. Income came only after the crops were harvested. During the rest of the year, farmers didn't have much cash income for months on end, but they needed money to buy seeds and equipment, hire help, and run the farm. In the absence of modern banking, they used loans on the cash value of their insurance policies to finance these expenses. In effect, the insurance company loaned the farmer money to get through to the harvest, and the farmer paid it back after the crops were sold.

Insurance started in churches to provide benefits to widows, then it transitioned into a savings vehicle. Then it became a vehicle for loans. Finally, these institutions evolved into the modern mutual life insurance company. They started investing the pooled money, making money on the investments, and then returning the profit to policyowners as dividends. All these benefits were added on to the central, foundational vehicle of an insurance policy that provided for the family by paying a death benefit.

Life insurance through a mutual company was a major vehicle for savings right up until the advent of the 401(k) in the 1980s. At that point, employees started to divert

money from life insurance into the stocl
investment-based vehicles, not savings vel

Life insurance became a lot less popular. It
method to save was drowned out by the barrage of promotion by financial institutions trying to sell you their
products. Insurance has become something that people
think is sold not bought, is expensive, and doesn't benefit
you so much as it benefits the person who's selling it to you.

The typical 401(k), IRA, and mutual funds compete with
life insurance for your money. They keep winning the
battle, even though they keep losing people's money,
charging high fees, and having scandal after scandal
after scandal.

INSURANCE AS THE FOUNDATION FOR WEALTH BUILDING

How do the wealthy use insurance differently than the
average person? It's not that the wealthy have all their
money in insurance. Rather, insurance is used as a foundational wealth vehicle by dynasties, executives, banks, and
corporations. The middle class aren't doing that. Author
Barry J. Dyke, in his book *Guaranteed Income,* writes that
Wall Street is the mechanism used by the elite to become
massively wealthy. The bulk of their assets come from
the middle class through their 401(k) contributions. The

contributions buy mutual funds to the tune of billions a year. Mutual funds use the money to buy stock in the companies the elite control. A seemingly infinite flow of money goes into their coffers, month in and month out. The profits and wealth that result are often stored in insurance products. For the wealthy, insurance fulfills multiple roles:

- **Traditional role of death payout.** The original purpose of insurance, dating back to the 1800s. If something unexpected happens, there's a payout.
- **Liquid assets in case of emergency.** Money withdrawn or loaned against the policy can be used for an unexpected event, such as a medical emergency or job loss.
- **Guaranteed loan provision.** You can borrow against the policy to take advantage of any purchase opportunity—including business, investment, or personal—that requires liquidity and fast action.

Insurance isn't an exclusive investment vehicle the way a 401(k) is. If you have a 401(k), you tie up your money, possibly for decades. To take advantage of a business opportunity, for instance, you'd have to find another source of capital, even though you might have enough money in your 401(k) to do the deal. But if you allocated the money you were previously saving in your 401(k) into a Wealth Maximization Account instead, you can have all its benefits, plus you can use the loan provision to take advantage of any number of opportunities. I often use the saying "When you have cash, opportunities seek you out."

PRIVATE VS. PUBLIC INSURANCE COMPANIES

Insurance was originally set up through private insurance companies that were organized as mutual companies. A mutual insurance company is owned by specific policyholders. It's a private company that is operated for profit—the profits go to providing benefits to the policyholders. If you own a participating policy in a mutual insurance company, you are a pro rata owner of the company. The responsibility and mission of the mutual company is to do what's best for their owners, the policyholders. The company is driven by this mission, which affects how it performs its fiduciary responsibilities, makes returns on the policyholders' money, makes business decisions—the whole agenda.

For many years, mutual companies such as Prudential, MetLife, and John Hancock were the main providers of life insurance. Starting in the 1990s, however, many of these companies demutualized. They converted themselves from being owned by the policyholders to being capital stock companies owned by shareholders. Instead of profits being distributed to the policyholders, the profits were now distributed to investors.

Private mutual insurance companies are not beholden to the demands of shareholders; their stewardship is to policyowners. When they make money, you make money in the form of a dividend.

INSURANCE AND TAXATION

"The only difference between death and taxes is that death doesn't get worse every time Congress meets."

—WILL ROGERS

The taxation of financial accounts and products is a key variable when weighing options to save and make an investment. Life insurance, as compared to alternatives, has some of the most lucrative tax benefits:

- **Beneficiaries.** The payout of life insurance to a beneficiary is income tax-free. It is estate-tax-free if the overall estate falls under a certain level.[62]
- **Cash Value.** The growth of cash value is tax-deferred, but with proper planning and foresight, can be used tax-free.
- **Policy Loans.** The funds received from a policy loan are not subject to income tax.
- **Withdrawals.** Withdrawals of cash value, called partial surrenders, are tax-free up to the basis (the overall amount contributed to the policy).

---

62   2018 exemption level is $11,180,000 for individuals and $22,360,000 for married couples.

THE HISTORY OF LIFE INSURANCE TAX TREATMENT

Into the 1980s, the 401(k) idea was just getting started, and individuals were still buying life insurance for savings. They were buying policies that had a cash value, because the tax treatment of these policies predated the Income Tax Act of 1913. Growth of cash value was never taxed as earned income, so people put a lot of money into life insurance policies. Additionally, the loan interest on policy loans was completely deductible, even on personal purchases.

TEFRA, DEFRA, AND TAMRA

Then came a series of laws in the 1980s that completely overhauled the tax code-TEFRA was passed in 1982, DEFRA in 1984, and TAMRA in 1988. Included in these laws were conditions that life insurance policies had to meet in order to qualify for its tax benefits. Some popular insurance products at that time, including single premium life insurance, were most affected by the new legislation.

SINGLE PREMIUM POLICIES

You can buy a single premium life insurance policy with one upfront payment. The cash value for these types of policies will typically be more than 90 percent of that initial, one-time payment in the first year. This cash value continues to earn dividends and interest each year and eventually exceeds the single premium paid by the third or fourth year.

The gains earned on the cash value on a single premium policy were tax-free for a long time. If you bought and funded a policy at a young age, the accumulated interest and dividends on it could have been substantial. These policies were popular because they were an ideal savings vehicle.

Congress passed the Technical and Miscellaneous Revenue Act of 1988 (TAMRA) to make the gains on single premium policies tax-deferred, not tax-free. This caused a slight disruption to how life insurance cash value growth was taxed. This led to the development of the twin sibling to single premium policies, the PUA rider. The PUA rider can be added to a whole life policy to create the same dynamic as the single premium policy.

HOW TO MAXIMIZE THE MODIFIED ENDOWMENT CONTRACT (MEC)

Since 1983, all life insurance policies have had a requirement called the 7-pay test. To understand this concept, start with the IRS's point of view: People were using flexible premium life insurance policies to buy policies that had very small death benefits. They would make a substantial upfront payment instead of paying yearly premiums, and then reap the tax benefits. Billions of dollars poured into life insurance every year because of this.

The IRS saw this as a tax shelter, not insurance, because the point of life insurance is the death benefit to replace the lost financial value of the insured. So, over the course of the 1980s, Congress passed several laws that changed the rules. Among other things, life insurance policies now had to pass the 7-pay test.

The 7-pay test is a formula created by the IRS to define how an insurance policy is taxed. The 7-pay test measures the amount of money that is paid into a policy over the course of seven years, relative to the amount of coverage or death benefit. If the death benefit is too low, the policy is taxed unfavorably.[63] If the death benefit is sufficient, the cash value grows tax-deferred and with the proper planning, accessed tax-free.

When you buy life insurance, the insurer looks at your age, sex, health rating, and coverage amount. Because everyone is different, each policy is individual to the purchaser and slightly different from any other policy. That's why each insurance policy ledger includes the dollar amount associated with the 7-pay test.

---

63   https://www.investopedia.com/terms/l/lifo.asp

Until the government clamped down, the single premium policy was attractive to millions of people for savings and wealth building. Those who purchased a policy before the ruling weren't affected, only those after. Today, you can set up a high cash value policy with a paid-up additions (PUA) rider. The majority of the PUA premium paid is immediate cash value, which earns interest and dividends. However, when adding the PUA rider, it must comply with parameters set by the 1980s legislation. The rules of the 7-pay test say if you contribute too much money into the rider, the policy becomes a modified endowment contract (MEC) and the tax treatment changes. How much is too much? This is a per-policy calculation to ensure that there's sufficient death benefit for the premium. If there's too much premium and not enough death benefit, then the policy is a MEC.

This chart illustrates the difference between single premium, 7-pay limit, basic whole life, and term insurance policies.

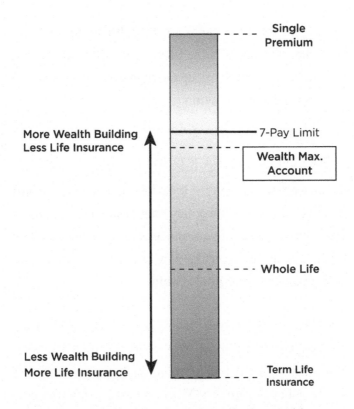

For the purposes that have been described up to this stage, you don't want this to happen to your policy, because the tax treatment of a MEC is such that you could end up paying a lot more tax on any distribution from it. If you don't follow the 7-pay rules, your life insurance policy can become a MEC almost without you noticing it. Strategically setting up this wealth building tool and compliance with all the regulations requires a trained professional. You want someone who both understands the role this type of policy plays in your finances and owns it themselves.

Paradigm Life[64] and our team of Wealth Strategists work with clients throughout the US to ensure that these invaluable tools are not only set up the right way but are suitable for your specific situation.

HOW TO FUND AN ACCOUNT

If you were to call up your local life insurance agent and ask to buy a whole life policy, they'd sell it to you, most likely based on the life insurance coverage you need. The cash value in the typical policy builds slowly over time and gives you a marginal benefit.

When you fund a Wealth Maximization Account, however, the purpose is different. Your objective is to establish high cash value for wealth building. The primary factor in the policy design is NOT the coverage—it's your contribution amount. Once this dollar amount is determined, also known as the premium, the coverage is as low as the MEC rules allow.

If your circumstances demand life insurance protection, that is taken into consideration and offered accordingly, typically by using term insurance that can be converted to a WMA in the future.

Most people think of life insurance as having a single-

---

64 www.paradigmlife.net

dimensional use—something you buy to protect your family in case you die prematurely. The purpose of the WMA, however, is to store cash and build wealth—which are *living benefits*.

The following image gives you an idea of the spectrum of premium amounts ranging from a low premium (10-year level term), to the highest premium (single-pay) as well as the 7-pay level, where you retain all the tax benefits.

The details of the example are as follows.

COMPARISON OF SINGLE PAY, 7-PAY, FULL PAY

- Age: 45
- Sex: Male
- Life Insurance Coverage Amount: $1,000,000

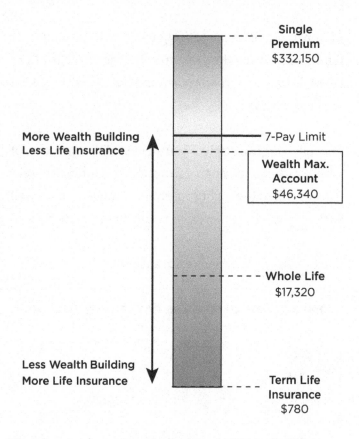

Single Premium $332,150

More Wealth Building Less Life Insurance

7-Pay Limit

Wealth Max. Account $46,340

Whole Life $17,320

Less Wealth Building More Life Insurance

Term Life Insurance $780

To reiterate, in a properly designed WMA, the life insurance coverage is minimal, and the contribution amount is close to the 7-pay threshold. When this is done, the policy performance is optimal.

The next images show how the different policies would illustrate out over the course of 50 years, based on current dividend schedules.

Single Premium				
Year	Age	Annual Premium	Cash Value	Death Benefit
1	46	$332,150	$306,330	$1,002,170
2	47		$319,516	$1,009,967
3	48		$333,210	$1,019,076
4	49		$457,481	$1,028,223
5	50		$362,328	$1,037,432
6	51		$377,782	$1,046,732
7	52		$393,844	$1,056,224
8	53		$410,516	$1,064,939
9	54		$427,825	$1,075,929
10	55		$445,752	$1,086,256
20	65		$664,493	$1,211,915
30	75		$963,524	$1,385,799
40	85		$1,344,513	$1,628,501
50	95		$1,734,008	$1,919,198

Wealth Max. Account				
Year	Age	Annual Premium	Cash Value	Death Benefit
1	46	$46,340	$35,813	$1,009,414
2	47	$46,340	$77,654	$1,010,550
3	48	$46,340	$127,040	$1,011,779
4	49	$46,340	$180,202	$1,013,613
5	50	$46,340	$237,034	$1,015,208
6	51	$46,340	$297,553	$1,096,487
7	52	$46,340	$362,159	$1,228,659
8	53		$384,553	$1,241,907
9	54		$408,305	$1,256,697
10	55		$433,459	$1,273,122
20	65		$775,189	$1,541,253
30	75		$1,351,600	$2,017,514
40	85		$2,255,535	$2,771,252
50	95		$3,508,482	$3,899,495

Whole Life				
Year	Age	Annual Premium	Cash Value	Death Benefit
1	46	$17,320	$0	$1,000,000
2	47	$17,320	$2,140	$1,000,000
3	48	$17,320	$18,360	$1,000,000
4	49	$17,320	$36,720	$1,001,570
5	50	$17,320	$54,580	$1,002,080
6	51	$17,320	$72,990	$1,002,610
7	52	$17,320	$92,850	$1,004,070
8	53	$17,320	$112,330	$1,004,690
9	54	$17,320	$132,330	$1,005,350
10	55	$17,320	$152,790	$1,006,070
20	65	$17,320	$356,280	$1,014,930
30	75	$17,320	$574,380	$1,023,350
40	85	$17,320	$773,830	$1,033,090
50	95	$17,320	$897,610	$1,036,000

10-Year Level Term				
Year	Age	Annual Premium	Cash Value	Death Benefit
1	46	$780	$0	$1,000,000
2	47	$780	$0	$1,000,000
3	48	$780	$0	$1,000,000
4	49	$780	$0	$1,000,000
5	50	$780	$0	$1,000,000
6	51	$780	$0	$1,000,000
7	52	$780	$0	$1,000,000
8	53	$780	$0	$1,000,000
9	54	$780	$0	$1,000,000
10	55	$780	$0	$1,000,000
20	65	$0	$0	$0
30	75	$0	$0	$0
40	85	$0	$0	$0
50	95	$0	$0	$0

The amount you put into your foundational asset, the WMA, is based on your specific financial situation. This is just an example.

You can start a small account on newborns for $50 to $100 per month (juvenile insurance), while wealthy families may buy many millions of dollars in policies. And remember, banks and corporations have billions in cash value across numerous insurance policies on their employees.

Insurance has evolved since the tax code changes of the 1980s. Life expectancies have gone up, so the mortality tables (actuarial data that show the incidence of death, by age, among groups of people) that determine what you'll pay for a policy based on your age have changed as well.

The insurance industry has adapted to tax code changes and longer lives. They've created whole life policies that can be utilized as ideal savings vehicles with optimal liquidity.

To set up one of these accounts, one way to determine the amount to contribute is by looking at a few things: your earned income, cash flow from investments, and cash on hand. Now, instead of your cash sitting in the bank, it will be earning more and will be accessible.

Your ongoing cash flow to accumulate more savings will

no longer sit in mutual funds or the market, where it's subject to loss. Instead, it will accumulate in what can be considered the bank account of the wealthy, where it earns tax-free dividends. If you have an opportunity or need liquidity, the money is available to you quickly and easily.

Let's look at another example. Assuming you have $25,000 in a liquid savings account set aside for emergencies and opportunities, and $12,000 per year that you are comfortable saving, this is how your WMA would look over time.

Year	Age	Annual Premium	Cash Value	Death Benefit
1	46	$37,000	$28,597	$793,152
2	47	$12,000	$37,380	$793,382
3	48	$12,000	$50,387	$793,629
4	49	$12,000	$64,541	$794,304
5	50	$12,000	$79,628	$794,730
6	51	$12,000	$95,680	$795,188
7	52	$12,000	$112,987	$795,919
8	53		$118,895	$773,180
9	54		$125,158	$751,769
10	55		$131,771	$731,592
20	65		$217,914	$580,389
30	75		$369,154	$584,398
40	85		$604,166	$758,505
50	95		$923,018	$1,033,259

In the specific situation shown in this example, the cash on hand goes into the policy as a one-time paid-up additions contribution and is liquid right away. The ongoing cash flow is broken into two parts: the base long-term whole life policy, and another annual PUA rider that has the same liquidity and wealth building benefits.

A policy structured in this way functions as your foundational asset. It earns interest and dividends tax-free. If you withdraw the money, you don't have to pay tax on the amount up to your basis, or the amount you have contributed. If you take a loan against it, you don't have to pay tax on the entire amount. When you pass away, the death benefit also passes to your heirs with efficient tax treatment.

HOW DO I SET UP A POLICY?

If you want to set up a policy, you can go on your own and find a mutual insurance company, insurance agent, or financial advisor who genuinely understands how to design a policy that best suits your situation and provides these benefits. Most mutual life insurance companies have independent representatives who are familiar with the concepts and will understand how to set up a policy for you. But it could take you months of calls and meetings to find the right company, the right representative, and the right policy. Even then, you might not end up with the best product.

Or you can contact my team. Our phone number is (855) 238-1833, and our email address is headsiwin@paradigmlife.net.

We offer complimentary video-based, online consultations so you don't even have to leave the comfort of your own home or office.

HOW MANY ACCOUNTS?

The IRS limits how much money you can put into savings vehicles like a 401(k), IRA, or a Roth IRA. With insurance, the IRS has created the 7-pay limit, which is a per-policy measurement. However, the actual limits on how many policies you can have are set by the insurance company, not the IRS. You can put a lot of money into policies, although the company won't insure your life for more than you are worth.

The whole idea of insurance is to replace a loss, and what's being lost is your future earned income potential, plus interest. The company actuaries have equations to calculate that figure, which varies depending on age, profession, education, and other factors. For instance, if you are 50 years old and your annual earned income is $100,000, the insurance company won't let you buy a policy for $10 million dollars. That amount of money would replace more than what your future income would have been.

Underwriting is the way an insurance company decides whether to accept your application for a policy and how much the policy should cost for insurance you require. The underwriters are the gatekeepers.

The underwriters are there to look out for the best interest of the insurance company's stockholders—its policyholders. They will insure you only if you fit into the models that are profitable to them. The underwriters look at a lot of standards to make the decision: underwriting standards, health standards, financial standards, and insurable interest standards. This benefits you as a policyowner as you receive a portion of company profits in the form of a dividend.

The insurable interest standard is important. You can take out insurance on anyone whose death would affect you financially. You can insure family members, business partners, employees, or anyone whose loss will inflict a justifiable financial loss on you. I own insurance on myself, my parents, my wife, my kids, and on some of my key employees.

But if I were to try to get insurance on my neighbor, I couldn't. I don't have an insurable interest in him—I would be sad if he died, but his death wouldn't affect me financially.

THE PRIVACY OF INSURANCE

Today, insurance is really the only private financial contract you have left. You're a private person, the mutual life company is a private company, and you therefore have a contract between two private parties. Nobody knows you have it unless you tell somebody. There's no public record, unlike bank accounts, brokerage accounts, or a 401(k).

A life insurance policy is a separate asset from corporate interests and business interests. It's protected anywhere there's going to be risk. Many states consider insurance a financial tool that is protected against bankruptcy or a lawsuit. Take the example of Kenneth Lay, the former chairman of Enron. He was convicted of fraud, but most of his assets and compensation package were in annuities and insurance. Because he lived in Texas, where these assets are protected against legal judgments, the assets went to his spouse after his untimely death and couldn't be touched.[65]

POLICY LOANS

The ability to borrow against your growing account value makes this financial tool extremely attractive. Most people only have one option for financing—banks. This tool gives you an alternative. The terms for a policy loan are by far the loosest lending terms, *period*. Here are the primary differences between private policy loans from the insurance company and a bank loan.

---

65 https://www.nytimes.com/2006/07/06/business/06legal.html; https://www.motherjones.
    com/politics/2002/02/ken-lays-nest-egg/; http://online.wsj.com/public/resources/
    documents/feb_7.htm

POLICY LOAN VS. TRADITIONAL BANK LOAN

INSURANCE COMPANY	BANK
No credit check with credit bureaus	Credit score qualification required
Private loan not on the UCC-1 reports[66]	Public information on the UCC-1 filing
Payment history does not show up on credit bureau reports	Payment history available on credit bureau reports
Interest-only with flexible payment provisions	Strict lending terms and payments
Loan limit is based on amount of cash value	Loan limit is based on collateral, credit score, and earned income amount
Access to money within days	Access to money based on the loan purpose— immediate to months

OTHER LOAN CONSIDERATIONS

- A policy loan does not have a specific term.
- You can pay interest only or defer all payments. The insurance company will bill you for the interest annually. If you have enough cash value left in the policy, they'll allow you to defer the payment without penalty.
- With a policy loan, you don't have to sacrifice the growth of your savings to take advantage of a business deal or other opportunity. With a loan outstanding, your cash value keeps growing.

OTHER TYPES OF LIFE INSURANCE

During the 1980s, a period of high interest rates and

---

66 https://en.wikipedia.org/wiki/UCC-1_financing_statement

volatility, insurance companies came up with what they considered a modern form of whole life insurance called universal life. Today, many of the original universal life policies have failed or sadly been converted to their derivatives, variable universal life and indexed universal life.

I have seen hundreds of these types of policies and have analyzed the mechanics, the economics, and the risks. I compare it to something that has already been covered in the book: when corporations shifted their risk with an employee pension to the employee using the 401(k).

The gains of these types of market-tied policies, as well as costs, lack the guarantees of the policies we use. They also afford insurance companies the right to adjust them if financial circumstances change. They shifted their risk to the policyowner.

These types of insurance policies do not align with the principles of this book, and I highly discourage you from using them.

I don't own them and don't sell them.

HOW INSURANCE BROKERS MAKE MONEY

There are two ways insurance brokers make money: upfront fees that are set by the insurance company, and annual servicing fees, usually a percentage of the pol amount. These servicing and marketing expenses a.c set up front when the policy is originally designed by the insurance company and are nonnegotiable.

Insurance companies don't typically have much customer service. Fees aren't based on the accumulation of the amount of cash value or policy size; they're based on the cash flows. Insurance is front-end loaded, in a sense, because there are limited expenses down the road, compared to a normal Exchange Traded Funds (ETF), mutual fund, or 401(k). By comparison, your mutual fund manager takes a fee every time money goes into your account, plus annual fees based on the total amount in the portfolio. Fees are charged whether the portfolio had a gain or loss. The fees may be small, but over the lifetime of your mutual fund investments, they add up to a huge amount of money. I will show you a comparison below.

Let's do an example based on the assumption that you pay a policy premium of $10,000 per year, set up for maximum cash value to the pre-set limitation of the IRC 7702:

Upfront fees:[67] When you contribute $10,000 to a policy designed as a WMA, it's typically broken into two parts—

---

67 Fees and commissions vary, depending the insurance company and their relationship to the broker and agent. The information presented is typical based on what the author has experienced.

the base whole life policy and the Paid-Up Additions rider. Let's assume the base whole life policy is $3,500 per year, and the Paid-Up Additions Rider is $6,500. The $3,500 base policy usually provides a one-time compensation to the servicing agent in the amount of 50 percent, or $1,750. Then, 50 percent also goes to the agency that the agent works with. The Paid-Up Additions rider pays 2.5 percent to the agent and 2.5 percent to the agency. I often refer to the compensation side of setting up these policies as the marketing expense, because the companies do little to no marketing to attract customers. Their marketing comes from their representatives. It's a one-time compensation fee when the account is first opened.

Annual servicing fees: Every year, the agent and agency receive a servicing fee based on your premium amount. It's usually 3 to 5 percent of the payment going to both the agent and the agency. Insurance companies do not have robust customer service departments and heavily rely on the agency and individual representatives to provide ongoing support of customers.

401(k) fees vs. insurance commissions: When you line up the 401(k) fee structure to the commissions predetermined by the insurance company, here are the results:

- Assumptions 401(k):
  - $10,000 contribution per year

- Performance based on the last 20 years of the S&P 500 Index[68]
- 1 percent management fee
- 1 percent administration fee
- **Total Fees: $49,758**

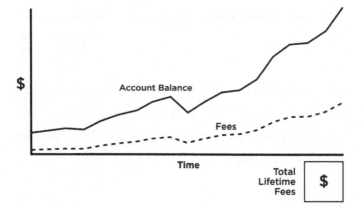

- Assumptions for WMA:
  - 20-year contribution period
  - Base premium: $3,500
  - PUA: $6,500
  - Commission structure as described
  - **Total Fees: $13,325**

---

68   Pinnacle Data Corp

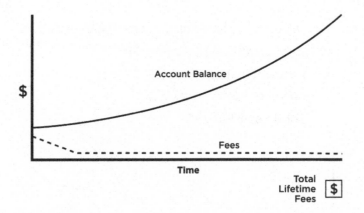

The 401(k) combined fees are 273 percent, or $36,433 more than the insurance policy. We have included the calculation breakdown of this example in *The Financial Strategy Study Guide*.

IS THIS APPROACH RIGHT FOR YOU?

I can't tie being a good candidate for a Wealth Maximization Account to a dollar amount of income. It's likely that if you're making six figures, you would want to seriously consider whether this approach is right for you. It's not a matter of how much surplus cash flow you have. It's more a financial state of mind. The WMA is a good choice if you're already financially responsible, are financially educated, have a strategy to grow wealth, and are disciplined enough to implement it. This product can help accelerate that growth. It could replace tools you're already using, such as a brokerage account, savings accounts, CDs, ETFs, or mutual funds.

However, if you're not financially disciplined and don't have a wealth-building strategy, buying any financial product (not just insurance) isn't going to help you—and may hurt you.

KEY TAKEAWAYS

- BE-DO-HAVE. The wealthy operate with a different mindset and use different financial tools and strategies. When you emulate them, you will experience similar results.
- Accumulating money is not sufficient to secure a financial future for you and your heirs. You need to educate your family about the financial principles you subscribe to.
- The greatest assets are people, relationships, and personal development.
- The purpose of a WMA is to store cash and build wealth.
- The idea isn't to have all your money in a life insurance policy, but rather to use it as a foundational asset for wealth building.
- Find a financial professional that understands how The Wealth Maximization Account works and owns one themselves.

CHAPTER 9

=====

MYTHS AND TRUTHS OF INSURANCE

"It ain't what you don't know that gets you into trouble. It's what you know for sure that just ain't so."

—MARK TWAIN

Our philosophy at Paradigm Life is to prove everything out and take away misconceptions and flawed information. We hear misconceptions about insurance all the time. A lot of them originate from Wall Street and the financial institutions that compete against insurance for your investment and savings.

Let's bust some myths.

MYTH: INSURANCE POLICIES ARE EXPENSIVE

One misleading claim is that insurance policies are expensive from an administrative perspective. In any analysis of what's expensive and what isn't, there must be a comparison. All financial tools have expenses—administrative, operational, marketing, sales commissions, and more—with the goal of winding up with a profit. If the company isn't profitable, it will go out of business. When it is profitable, the profits must go somewhere. That's the best starting place to determine whether a financial tool is expensive or not, especially this one.

A MUTUAL INSURANCE COMPANY IS RUN TO BE PROFITABLE TO YOU

The profit is for the benefit of its policyholders, not to pay huge bonuses to the C-suite or dividends to shareholders. Any company will have expenses and overhead, but at the end of the year, a mutual insurance company is always profitable. Those profits are distributed to policyowners in the form of a dividend—there are no excess expenses beyond what the company needs to operate.

A mutual insurance company has a board of directors chosen by the policyholders. The fiduciary responsibility of any board of directors is to do what's in the best interest of the owners of the company—the policyowners. The board has a directive, a vision, a clear mission.

**NEW YORK LIFE STATEMENT
FROM ANNUAL REPORT**

The performance turned in by our team of agents and employees resulted in record financial strength. In a year when the company grew stronger than ever before—and despite the low interest rate environment—we were able to pay out the largest dividend in company history. Throughout 2017, we will distribute $1.77 billion back to our eligible policyowners. This marks our 163rd year of paying a dividend.[69]

MYTH: INSURANCE COMPANIES AREN'T SAFE

Mutual insurance companies are extremely safe. Your money is secure when you put it into a life insurance company. The business model for insurance is actuarial science—the profit for an insurance company is based on extremely accurate mathematical models. Actuarial science tells a life insurance company exactly how much money it will need to pay out each year in insurance claims. The profit for insurance companies is designed not by a probability, but by an inevitability. Some highly predictable number of the people covered by their insurance will die each year. Everything the company does is based on that knowledge.

69 https://www.newyorklife.com/content/dam/nyl-cms-dotcom/pdfs/financial-info/2016/2016-Annual-Report.pdf

Insurance companies are highly regulated at the state and federal level. Among many other strict requirements, they must have enough regulated, liquid assets in reserve to pay 100 percent of the present value of claims.

Rating agencies such as A.M. Best, S&P, and Moody's constantly analyze and rank insurance company stability and are quick to spot problems with a company's assets. Each state has a guaranty association that acts as a safety net for policyholders in case an insurer becomes insolvent. It's as if every single state has its own FDIC. The amounts each state will cover are regulated by the state insurance department. They vary a bit from state to state (you can check online for your state[70]) but generally cover the value of most policies. Regulators can almost always spot a company in trouble well in advance of insolvency and force it to take steps, including selling itself to another insurer, to correct any problems.

THE INSURANCE INDUSTRY IS SEPARATE FROM THE FINANCIAL INDUSTRY

The insurance industry is very different from the rest of the financial industry. Insurance companies aren't highly leveraged like other financial institutions. If there's a stock market collapse or big adjustment, the insurance industry is typically prepared and resilient. The money

---

70 https://www.nolhga.com/policyholderinfo/main.cfm

you have in your policies isn't affected by stock market movement. In fact, when the stock market goes through a big adjustment, guess who swoops in and buys up assets at a great price? Insurance companies.

To take just one great example, in the 2003–2004 recession, right after the dot.com bubble, a mutual company wrote a check for $100 million for a couple of parcels of land on Boston Harbor.[71] That's a whole lot of money to have on hand, but they had it because they had liquidity, they are institutional investors, and they understand opportunities. They later sold part of the development for over $1.1 billion.[72]

Most insurance companies, if they wanted to go out of business, could pay off every single policyowner with their assets and probably give each a bonus as well. That's not something a bank or financial institution could do—they don't have that kind of money on hand. In fact, since 2008, over 500 banks have failed.[73] Over that same period of time, only 17 insurance companies failed, none of which were mutual life insurance companies. Very few insurance companies go out of business.[74]

71 https://www.falloncompany.com/projects/fan-pier/

72 https://www.bizjournals.com/boston/real_estate/2014/05/sold-joe-fallon-s-two-vertex-buildings-on-fan-pier.html

73 https://en.wikipedia.org/wiki/List_of_bank_failures_in_the_United_States_(2008%E2%80%93present)

74 https://www.nolhga.com/factsandfigures/main.cfm/location/insolvencies

PUBLICLY TRADED INSURANCE COMPANIES MAY BE RISKY

Mutual insurance companies are very safe. Publicly traded insurance companies are a bit risky. These stock companies are still highly regulated and get the same scrutiny from outside rating agencies, but their allegiance isn't to you, the person who's buying an insurance policy. They make short-term decisions to appease existing and potentially new shareholders by showing optimistic quarterly earnings. Their allegiance is to their shareholders, who want profits above all else. If the company can't deliver on this short-term basis, the stockholders are going to sell or not buy.

Look at the people running the company at the highest echelon. They have a lot of their bonuses, retirement plans, and benefits packages in stock options. They want the company stock to be high; they're not going to purposefully figure out ways to lose value. They're going to be tempted to boost the stock price with gimmicks. That's how the insurance giant AIG—the biggest insurer in the world—came very close to default in the crash of 2008 and had to be bailed out by the government to the tune of $85 billion. AIG insured collateralized debt obligations that included bonds that funded subprime mortgages.[75] They made a lot of money doing this—until the credit market started crashing and they had to make

75   https://www.investopedia.com/terms/c/cdo.asp

good on their insurance obligations. AIG was on the hook for way more money than they had.[76] After the bailout, AIG returned to profitability and in 2017 was taken off the government's list of companies considered too big to fail. The problems AIG experienced would likely not have happened with a mutual company.

MYTH: I'M TOO OLD

A lot of my clients think they're too old to buy life insurance. Age doesn't have much to do with the decision. We've done business with people over 80. Wealth strategy differs by individual. Someone over 60 typically isn't focused on long-term objectives; someone who's 30 isn't focused on turning all their assets into cash flow. Rather than looking at an age number, look at the larger goal and how the WMA improves it.

That said, if you're older (let's say in your 60s), the value of the policy is twofold. First, it becomes your legacy asset to be passed on to your heirs, as well as a location of certainty for your cash. Second, it acts as a permission slip to maximize cash flow from the other assets you have accumulated, such as your retirement accounts, primary residence, rental property equity, business interests, and so on. If you can figure out a way to write a check for the last of your money on your deathbed, have fun. By the

---

76   https://www.wsj.com/articles/u-s-rescinds-federal-oversight-of-aig-1506722576

time you die, you're most likely either going to be short of money or have too much. If you're short right now, somebody else has to pay for you. These strategies make sure you don't spend all your wealth by the time you pass away. (The details of two of our income strategies will be covered in detail in Chapter Twelve.)

MYTH: LOW RATE OF RETURN

To become wealthy, it is best to observe and consider emulating where the wealthy and successful institutions protect and grow their capital. Big corporations like Walmart, GE, and banks own billions of dollars of high cash value insurance on their employees, because they have insurable interest in them. In fact, a lot of banks have huge amounts of cash value because it qualifies for their Tier 1 capital requirement—their core capital.[77] It's a way to store money, earn a tax favorable return, and have access to the cash value when they need it.[78]

The primary role of a Wealth Maximization Account is important to understand when evaluating its rate of return.

Whole life insurance has a low rate of return is a concern raised by many of our clients. The typical financial advi-

---

77   https://www.investopedia.com/terms/t/tier1capital.asp

78   http://www.equiasalliance.com/images/PDFs/boli-holdings-reports/Q4-2017-BOLI-
     Holdings-Report.pdf; http://www.bolicoli.com/; https://www.investopedia.com/terms/b/boli.
     asp; https://www.investopedia.com/terms/c/coli.asp

sor usually dismisses the strategy saying it doesn't return enough money. My response is usually, "Well, compared to what? What does *enough* mean?" To answer these questions, there must be something to compare it to.

The Wealth Maximization Account is best categorized with a savings account, CD, or money market account because of its guarantees. The account guarantees are backed up by the insurance company and its assets and a state guaranty association,[79] similar to the protection FDIC provides to bank accounts.

For nearly a decade, savings accounts, CDs, and money market accounts at banks have been paying historically low yields.[80] These accounts are all taxable at ordinary income tax rates.

The internal rate of return (IRR) of a Wealth Maximization Account is also at historic lows, with a range of 4 to 6 percent.[81] The IRR is the projection used when illustrating the net return on future values over a long-term time frame.

I included a video tutorial in *The Financial Strategy Study*

---

79 https://www.acli.com/Industry-Facts/Guaranty-Associations; https://www.investopedia.com/terms/i/insurance-guaranty-association.asp

80 http://www.forecast-chart.com/rate-cd-interest.html

81 30-year internal rate of return of cash value, under 60 years of age. 30-year internal rate of return on death benefit.

Guide that walks you through the step-by-step design of a Wealth Maximization Account, which illustrates the IRR and what a comparable savings account yield would need to be (headsortailsiwin.com/StudyGuide).

Highlighted in the tutorial is a performance that compares more to an investment than a guaranteed savings account, precluding the risk of loss.

If you compare the performance of a WMA to a long-term investment in the stock market, it will surprise you. When you factor taxes, fees, and inflation into a market-based investment, you don't end with much more than you started with. The money you put into mutual funds for your 401(k) isn't available to you unless you pay a high penalty—then fees soak up some of the gain, and inflation eats away at your nest egg. The cash value of your WMA, on the other hand, is liquid; you can use the cash now. In the long term, your cash value is subject to inflation as well, but in the short term, you can use the money to take advantage of opportunities.

The WMA plays the role of your savings, emergency account, and opportunity fund. After you establish a sufficient reserve, you can leverage the loan provision and invest in other assets—it's the *and* asset, not a choice between one asset *or* another. This isn't the case with a savings account, CD, money market account, and investments, which are *or* assets.

EXPANDING ON MARKET RETURNS

In Chapter Four, the performance of the stock market was addressed and the corresponding flaws and reasoning for being a risky asset class for passive investors were exposed. I believe it is appropriate to expand on those points here.

A financial advisor will tell you that the rate of return of a stock market-based portfolio over the past 20, 30, or 40 years is 10 to 12 percent. These statements are rarely qualified, as most of us have not been taught how to check the math. In my experience, even advisors don't know how to check it.

Unfortunately, the values used in today's illustrations of a WMA don't reflect the actual long-term history of their dividends, which are much higher.[82] The dividends have varied over the years. The last several years have been some of the lowest dividend scales in history—yet the returns still measure better than a stock market-based portfolio or retirement account. If you then factor in all I've explained about taxes, fees, and inflation, your return over 30 years would still be higher than the stock market— and without the volatility that can wreck it.

---

82 www.headsortailsiwin.com/StudyGuide

Insurance versus stocks isn't always an apples-to-apples comparison. Even when the stock market is up, life insurance beats the best years in the stock market. What most advisors and talking heads say is, "Well, the market has done 10 to 12 percent per year." But those figures don't take cash flows into consideration. There's a huge difference between something earning a flat 10 percent compounded and earning an average 10 percent in a fluctuating market over the last 30 years. In fact, even though life insurance and stocks have about the same average annual return, the stock market return is sometimes 20 to 30 percent less money.

Let's go back to a concept in Chapter Four. Imagine you have $100,000 in the stock market, and you earn 100 percent on the money one year, then lose 50 percent of that the next year. Your average rate of return is 25 percent. But what do you wind up with? You started with $100,000 and doubled it to $200,000. Then you lost half of your money. Now you have $100,000 again, even though your average return was 25 percent.

Average Return: 25.00%			Actual Return: 0.00%	
Year	Beg. of Year Acct. Value	Earnings Rate	Interest Earnings	End of Year Acct. Value
1	100,000	100.00%	100,000	200,000
2	200,000	(50.00%)	(100,000)	100,000
3	100,000	100.00%	100,000	200,000
4	200,000	(50.00%)	(100,000)	100,000

Let's expand the example by analyzing the last 30 years of the Dow Jones Industrial Average.

Assumptions:

- 1988 to 2017
- $10,000 annual investment
- 1 percent total fees
- 20 percent blended tax rate

	Average Return: 9.71%			Actual Return: 4.96%			
Year	Beg. of Year Acct. Value	Earnings Rate	Annual Savings	Interest Earnings	Taxes	Misc. Fees	End of Year Acct. Value
1988		6.42%	10,000	642	(107)	(106)	10,429
1989	10,429	31.03%	10,000	6,339	(1,214)	(268)	25,286
1990	25,286	(7.10%)	10,000	(2,505)		(328)	32,453
1991	32,453	21.52%	10,000	9,135	(1,724)	(516)	49,348
1992	49,348	4.31%	10,000	2,559	(388)	(619)	60,900
1993	60,900	13.52%	10,000	9,585	(1,756)	(805)	77,925
1994	77,925	2.18%	10,000	1,916	(204)	(898)	88,739
1995	88,739	34.88%	10,000	34,443	(6,622)	(1,332)	125,228
1996	125,228	24.43%	10,000	33,041	(6,272)	(1,683)	160,315
1997	160,315	23.63%	10,000	40,250	(7,629)	(2,106)	200,831
1998	200,831	15.31%	10,000	32,272	(5,968)	(2,431)	234,704
1999	234,704	23.66%	10,000	57,903	(10,975)	(3,026)	288,606
2000	288,606	(6.26%)	10,000	(18,703)		(2,799)	277,104
2001	277,104	(5.38%)	10,000	(15,446)		(2,717)	268,941
2002	268,941	(14.55%)	10,000	(40,592)		(2,383)	235,966
2003	235,966	20.94%	10,000	51,503	(9,706)	(2,975)	284,789
2004	284,789	3.07%	10,000	9,050	(1,202)	(3,038)	299,598
2005	299,598	1.10%	10,000	3,404	(55)	(3,130)	309,818
2006	309,818	15.00%	10,000	47,973	(8,859)	(3,678)	355,254
2007	355,254	4.56%	10,000	16,673	(2,571)	(3,819)	375,537
2008	375,537	(30.74%)	10,000	(118,501)		(2,670)	264,365
2009	264,365	17.15%	10,000	47,048	(8,767)	(3,214)	309,433
2010	309,433	10.27%	10,000	32,800	(5,856)	(3,522)	342,855
2011	342,855	6.23%	10,000	21,969	(3,644)	(3,748)	367,432
2012	367,432	8.19%	10,000	30,906	(5,365)	(4,083)	398,890
2013	398,890	22.58%	10,000	92,335	(17,465)	(5,012)	478,748
2014	478,748	8.46%	10,000	41,369	(7,214)	(5,301)	517,602
2015	517,602	(3.84%)	10,000	(20,238)		(5,074)	502,291
2016	502,291	15.94%	10,000	81,638	(15,140)	(5,939)	572,849
2017	572,849	24.86%	10,000	144,886	(27,522)	(7,277)	692,936
Totals		9.71%	300,000	633,658	(156,223)	(84,499)	692,936

Results = $692,936

Actual Return = 4.96 percent

If you deferred your capital gains to 2017 and sold your position, your portfolio balance would be $892,391. After a 20 percent capital gains tax, the balance would be $713,912—an actual return of 5.1 percent. I go through these calculations in a video tutorial in *The Financial Strategy Study Guide*.

KEY TAKEAWAYS

- The wealthy approach things differently: their businesses, their decisions, their relationships, their opportunities. Their success is based on the utilization of financial tools, including insurance. The wealthy use the various benefits of insurance as the ideal storage place for their money. This insurance lets them use the highly flexible policy loan to follow opportunities. Therefore, we call the unique structure of a whole life policy The Wealth Maximization Account.

- Insurance can be used to mirror traditional accounts like 401(k), 403(b), 529 plans, and typical savings accounts—with several additional benefits that those tools do not offer.

- If you're a business owner or investor, you can use insurance in place of your opportunity fund—money you put in savings in preparation for finding deals.

- Insurance is the asset of choice to pass on to the next generation, which allows you a lot more flexibility with the other assets you've accumulated.

Insurance stands up to the test of time. It offers tax favorability, privacy, liquidity, and the safety of a guaranteed contract. It's managed by sound institutions. And as I'll explain in the next chapter, insurance lets you save and borrow smarter.

CHAPTER 10

SAVE, BORROW, INVEST, AND BUILD WEALTH

"Money is only a tool. It will take you wherever you wish, but it will not replace you as the driver."

—AYN RAND

The Perpetual Wealth Strategy combines education, financial tools, and investments to strategically increase your earned income, cash flow, and control, with the aim of achieving financial freedom as soon as possible.

If you're a real estate investor, the strategy gives you a superior yield on your liquid savings and access to additional leverage to enhance the overall performance of your portfolio.

For the executive, it replaces your 401(k) or can complement it by providing no annual limits on what you can contribute.

For families, it provides superior growth, liquidity, and control over a 529 plan.

For business owners, it offers unmatchable privacy and asset protection, while still giving you control to purchase equipment, finance your growth, and provide operating capital if needed. You can convert your existing key man, buy-sell, or stock redemption policies, as well as provide incentives to your executives using IRC 162 instead of a 401(k) or profit-sharing plan.

For those 50 years and older and planning on "retirement" within 15 years, it accelerates that time frame to as little as five years by positioning assets to generate guaranteed income, maximize Social Security benefits, minimize income tax, and establish long-term care protection, all within the same strategy. Many of you at this age can be financially free right now.

In Chapter Seven, I talked about Abraham Maslow and his Hierarchy of Needs. I apply the same logic for investing. I call it The Hierarchy of Wealth.

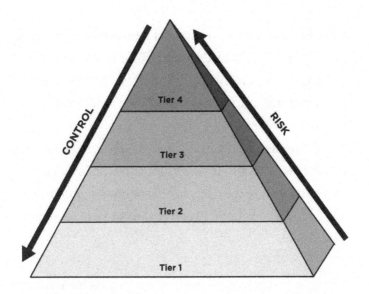

The first step is to build your foundation or Tier 1, which is often referred to as your reserve, your sleep-well-at-night account, or your rainy-day fund. I recommend putting aside 10 to 30 percent of your earned income in this tier and accumulating enough to cover at least six months of your expenses. I typically hold a minimum of 12 months' worth of personal expenses there. Hold up to 40 percent of your total assets in this tier.

After the foundation is poured, every dollar above and beyond that is the *opportunity fund*, where your investment capital originates. The second tier of investment consists of assets you control. Examples of this type of asset include, first, you. Your investment in personal development, certification, training courses, or paid mastermind groups helps to maximize your earning potential.

Investment real estate that meets certain criteria (covered in this chapter), and investment in your business (covered in Chapter Eleven), also falls into this category. I recommend putting 30 to 40 percent of your assets in Tier 2.

Tier 3 consists of assets that have collateral, but you don't control them. Examples are syndicated funds that invest in oil and gas, real estate, life settlements, and private lending. I recommend putting 20 to 30 percent of your assets here.

Tier 4, the final tier, is made of assets that have no collateral and that you don't control, often referred to as speculative investment. Mutual funds, exchange traded funds, and company stock all fall into this category. I recommend putting no more than 5 to 10 percent here.

The cash value of a properly funded whole life insurance policy is the ideal Tier 1 asset. You are able to save money and borrow it smarter, without involving a bank. That's why I call it The Wealth Maximization Account.

Instead of putting money into a bank account, CD, or mutual fund, which is what most people do, allocate your cash and savings to pay premiums into the same place where banks store their cash. The Wealth Maximization Account is your turbo-charged savings account and opportunity fund.

When an opportunity arises, instead of liquidating your account to make the investment or purchase, you borrow from the insurance company to make the investment. Your cash continues to grow, and you also have the investment.

Let's analyze a simple example.

Let's assume that your cash value amount is $100,000. Your reserve requirement to let you sleep well at night is $50,000, which leaves you with $50,000 as an opportunity fund.

Let's assume you choose a Tier 2 investment that pays a 15 percent cash flow per year.

Here is how it works out at the 10-year mark.

Your $100,000 of cash value would grow by 4 to 6 percent, but let's be conservative and say 4 percent. That's $48,024 of tax-free gain.

Present Value:	100,000
Annual Payment:	0.00
Annual Int. Rate:	4.00%
Years:	10
Future Value:	148,024

The loan from the insurance company to make the investment would be at 5 percent. Let's say it's paid back with 100 percent of the investment cash flow, 15 percent, which is $625 per month.

Loan Balance:	(50,000.00)
Monthly Payment:	625.00
Annual Int. Rate:	5.00%
Future Value:	0
Months:	97.51

The loan would be paid off in the 98th month; however, the cash flow from the investment would still be flowing in. Once the loan is repaid, that $625 per month would go into the WMA, earning 4 percent, and grow to $14,571.

Present Value:	0.00
Monthly Payment:	625.00
Annual Int. Rate:	4.00%
Months:	22.49
Future Value:	14,571

Here's how the numbers work out in the end:

Start

$100,000 Cash Value

- $50,000 allocated as reserve
- $50,000 allocated as opportunity fund

Investment

$50,000 paying 15 percent ($625 per month)

Gain

+ $48,024 from dividends and interest earned on the $100,000 cash value

+ $14,571 of additional cash value from the investment cash flow added to the WMA

= $62,595 total gain after 10 years

How does that compare to the standard investment most people would make with the same $100,000? Most would allocate $50,000 to the investment and keep $50,000 in savings.

Here's how the numbers work out:

With $50,000 in savings earning a taxable 0.5 percent, let's assume a 33 percent marginal tax bracket. The gain would be $1,700 over 10 years.

Year	Beg. of Year Acct. Value	Earnings Rate	Interest Earnings	Taxes	End of Year Acct. Value
1	50,000	0.50%	250	(83)	50,168
2	50,168	0.50%	251	(83)	50,336
3	50,336	0.50%	252	(83)	50,504
4	50,504	0.50%	253	(83)	50,673
5	50,673	0.50%	253	(84)	50,843
6	50,843	0.50%	254	(84)	51,013
7	51,013	0.50%	255	(84)	51,184
8	51,184	0.50%	256	(84)	51,356
9	51,356	0.50%	257	(85)	51,528
10	51,528	0.50%	258	(85)	51,700
Totals		0.50%	2,538	(838)	51,700

The $625 per month or $7,500 per year investment cash flow from the investment would also go back into savings and grow to $76,396 (after tax) over 10 years.

Year	Beg. of Year Acct. Value	Earnings Rate	Annual Cash Flow	Interest Earnings	Taxes	End of Year Acct. Value
1		0.50%	7,500	38	(12)	7,525
2	7,525	0.50%	7,500	75	(25)	15,075
3	15,075	0.50%	7,500	113	(37)	22,651
4	22,651	0.50%	7,500	151	(50)	30,252
5	30,252	0.50%	7,500	189	(62)	37,879
6	37,879	0.50%	7,500	227	(75)	45,531
7	45,531	0.50%	7,500	265	(88)	53,208
8	53,208	0.50%	7,500	304	(100)	60,912
9	60,912	0.50%	7,500	342	(113)	68,641
10	68,641	0.50%	7,500	381	(126)	76,396
Totals		0.50%	75,000	2,083	(688)	76,396

The combined amount of money in the end would be:

+ $1,700 from interest earned on the savings account

+ $76,396 from investment cash flow

- $50,000 initial investment

= $28,096 total gain after 10 years

The difference in strategy is as follows:

Option 1: Using The Wealth Maximization Account: $62,595

Option 2: Using the typical approach: $28,096

Advantage of using The Wealth Maximization Account = $34,499

ERIK'S STORY

Now, let's look at a real-life example of how this might work. The period of 2009–2011 was filled with a lot of sad stories. Many of them ended up being blessings in disguise. My client Erik already had a whole life policy when we met, but the design was insufficient based on his earned income and assets. We set up additional, more appropriate policies on Erik and his wife.

A few years before, Erik made a Tier 4 investment in a private investment fund that came crashing down in the financial crisis. He knew that the fund still had assets, so he hired an attorney to pursue the fund manager. The attorney was able to get a judgment against the fund manager, and Erik was able to take control of the assets. The main asset of the failed fund was an apartment in a Miami high-rise. At one point, it was worth $2 million, but because of the crisis, it was now valued at only $450,000. The assets of the fund were going to be distributed to all the investors as a settlement. When we ran the numbers, we realized that it would be a good idea to buy out the other investors with cash. Because he had liquidity and his money was readily accessible through a policy loan from his insurance company, Erik was able to get the cash he needed to buy out the interest of the other investors. The economic environment was perfect to negotiate, especially since he had cash immediately available.

Erik ended up as the sole owner of the apartment. He rented it out for a few years until the market improved. In 2013, he sold the condo for over $1 million.

Whole life insurance gives you the ability to access cash and deploy it when an opportunity arises—and this was clearly an amazing opportunity. Because Erik had that cash, he was able to write the check within a few days, take ownership of the condo, and eventually sell it and make a killing.

THE RATE OF RETURN ON QUICK CASH

Because you can access the cash value of your policy almost immediately, the money can be used for business purposes without involving a bank. A couple of my clients have used their policies to provide collateral for a bond. Of course, the bonding company must agree to this, but because they typically underwrite bonds on a case-by-case basis, they usually do. They see the policy as a very valuable asset.

One client is in the construction business. Contractors typically have to be bonded, and you need to put up collateral to get the bond. He was able to use the cash value of his policy as collateral instead of putting up his house or savings.

Another client was involved in a large lawsuit and needed to put up a substantial bond. Instead of withdrawing money from her retirement account or using cash on hand, she was able to get the bond company to use her insurance policy as collateral.

An example I share often is a great deal I got on a beautiful Jeep Wrangler because I had cash. One of the guys at the gym I belong to was getting married. His fiancée was insistent that he sell his Jeep before the wedding. She was much shorter than he and had a difficult time hoisting herself up into the Jeep—she often scuffed her clothes. The week of the wedding came, and they had a big blow-up because he still hadn't sold it. The four-door Jeep Wrangler was jet black, had big tires, and low mileage. At the time, it was worth about $35,000. I offered him $20,000 on the spot and said I would have a check the next day. Normally, the processing time for a loan from the insurance company is three to five days, but often they can wire or EFT the money the same day. He jumped at the offer.

I love Jeeps, but I love my wife more. Just as my friend discovered, my wife scuffed her clothes getting in. She despised the Jeep. I drove it for almost two years and then sold it for just under $30,000.

USING YOUR WMA TO PURCHASE INVESTMENT REAL ESTATE

Over the years, of the thousands of investments I have analyzed, the ones I have seen perform the best and most consistently are real estate related. A good friend and client of mine, Jason Hartman, has a popular podcast called *The Creating Wealth Show* that boasts hundreds of episodes and millions of downloads. Jason is one of the most informed people in the real estate world and has taught me directly and through his podcast the ideal criteria for a successful real estate investment. I firmly believe that everyone should own as many residential investment properties as they can, if they meet these criteria:

- Rent to value ratio of 1 percent ($100,000 home = $1,000 gross monthly rent)
- Mortgage the house at 75 to 80 percent of its value
- Home fits the median home price for the area
- At least three bedrooms and two bathrooms
- Have a property manager
- House has been recently updated

To learn more about areas of the country that meet these criteria, Jason's company Platinum Properties is a great resource.[83] We also have other resources like these in *The Financial Strategy Study Guide.*

---

83 https://www.jasonhartman.com/tag/platinum-properties

Buying and selling property this way is an incredible way to establish cash flow and hedge yourself against the economic forces of inflation. I have many clients who have achieved financial freedom through this model. Opportunities to purchase real estate this way are always popping up, but you need to know where to look and have the ability to access quick cash. I teach two primary strategies for acquiring property:

1. The down payment of 20 to 25 percent is made by borrowing from your insurance company against your WMA. The cash flow from property then goes to pay down your policy loan.
2. If you have enough cash value in your WMA, you can buy the property with cash within a few days. An immediate cash offer is often more attractive to sellers because they usually want to close and get their money as soon as possible. Sometimes a bank mortgage can take up to 60 days or longer. Once you purchase the property, you can then apply for a traditional mortgage at the 75 to 80 percent level.

In addition to this bread and butter model, other types of real estate deals become available when you have cash and liquidity. A good example is the story of my client Donald.

Donald owns and operates a successful software company in Michigan. He had moved to Oregon and flew back one week a month to handle whatever business needed to be done in person. He would stay at a hotel or with family for the week, but that arrangement was very cumbersome. During one visit, he happened to learn about a condo in a nearby gated community that was being sold at auction that month because the owner had defaulted. Michigan developed a poor reputation during the financial crisis, so many out-of-state investors stayed away. However, my client knew the area well and understood the numbers behind the deal.

He was able to borrow against his WMA to act quickly and buy the condo, which at its peak was worth over half a million dollars. He picked it up at the auction for just $100,000. He now uses it as a company condo instead of staying at a hotel, so he gets even more tax benefits.

During the last financial crisis, housing took a substantial hit. However, if your property met the criteria above, you came through the crisis. Your equity may have declined slightly, but the rental demand pushed cash flow up and vacancy rates down. And eventually prices and equity came back.

ESTABLISH A CHILD'S FINANCIAL FUTURE

The innate drive I have as a parent to teach, influence, and leave a legacy for my children was unexpected. It was sparked at the hospital when they were born and hasn't stopped.

While I was growing up, I wasn't taught much about money, investing, business, and entrepreneurship. I had to learn a lot of painful lessons. I have been fortunate to establish a financial system from which my kids are already benefiting. It's not the traditional financial system parents and grandparents used to save for their kids' future.

The 529 plan, also called a qualified tuition plan, is a tax-advantaged savings plan designed to encourage saving for future college costs. These plans are very popular and have become a sacred cow, even though they have only been around since 1996. When my two girls were born, my dad was insistent on contributing to a 529 plan for college. At the time, I was barely into my first job out of college and hadn't learned what I teach now, so we decided to open one up.

Today, millions of people have them, and your kids and grandkids are attached to them. In my experience, saying *no* to a 529 plan is like telling a mother her baby is ugly.

I don't want to say what you're doing is bad. You're planning for your child or grandchild's financial well-being, which is commendable. But if you look at the nature of a 529 plan, it's not set up for your best interests or the best interests of the child or grandchild. It's pitched to you as a benefit, but it's just another way for Wall Street to sell you mutual funds and make money off your desire to do well by your kids.

The objective of the 529 plan is to put money away and pay for future college expenses while getting a tax benefit for doing so. The catch is, if the money is not used for college or some other qualified higher education expense, you have to pay penalties for withdrawing it. What if you don't need the account anymore—your kid decides to skip college, for instance—and want to use that money for something else? Is the penalty you pay on the 529 plan worth it from the beginning?

Additionally, the burden on families to fund college completely has an opportunity cost that is difficult to quantify. Because of that, the financial future of the family may be put in jeopardy. I have seen it bankrupt a few.

Here's an example of what I mean. Assume your child is five years old and you have committed to taking care of their educational costs for a four-year degree.

Right now, the average annual cost to attend a public university is $25,000, rising by 5 percent a year.[84] That

---

84 https://trends.collegeboard.org/college-pricing/figures-tables/
    average-estimated-undergraduate-budgets-2017-18

means that by the time a five-year-old today is 18 and ready to go to college, tuition would be almost $50,000. Over four years, factoring in tuition rises, that comes to a total cost of $213,344.

For a 529 account to pay out that much when it's needed, it has to start with $100,000 and earn a net 5 percent every year through graduation.

Age	Year	Beg. of Year Acct. Value	Earnings Rate	Tuition Expense	Interest Earnings	End of Year Acct. Value
1	5	100,000	5.00%		5,000	105,000
2	6	105,000	5.00%		5,250	110,250
3	7	110,250	5.00%		5,513	115,763
4	8	115,763	5.00%		5,788	121,551
5	9	121,551	5.00%		6,078	127,628
6	10	127,628	5.00%		6,381	134,010
7	11	134,010	5.00%		6,700	140,710
8	12	140,710	5.00%		7,036	147,746
9	13	47,746	5.00%		7,387	155,133
10	14	155,133	5.00%		7,757	162,890
11	15	162,890	5.00%		8,144	171,034
12	16	171,034	5.00%		8,552	179,586
13	17	179,586	5.00%		8,979	188,565
14	18	188,565	5.00%		9,428	197,993
15	19	197,993	5.00%	(49,498)	7,425	155,920
16	20	155,920	5.00%	(51,973)	5,197	109,144
17	21	109,144	5.00%	(54,572)	2,729	57,301
18	22	57,301	5.00%	(57,301)	0	0
Totals			5.00%	(213,344)	113,344	0

Or, you could just save $8,147 a year for 18 years.

Age	Year	Beg. of Year Acct. Value	Earnings Rate	Tuition Payments	Annual Savings	Interest Earnings	End of Year Acct. Value
1	5	0	5.00%		(8,147)	407	8,555
2	6	8,555	5.00%		(8,147)	835	17,537
3	7	17,537	5.00%		(8,147)	1,284	26,968
4	8	26,968	5.00%		(8,147)	1,756	36,872
5	9	36,872	5.00%		(8,147)	2,251	47,270
6	10	47,270	5.00%		(8,147)	2,771	58,188
7	11	58,188	5.00%		(8,147)	3,317	69,652
8	12	69,652	5.00%		(8,147)	3,890	81,689
9	13	81,689	5.00%		(8,147)	4,492	84,328
10	14	94,328	5.00%		(8,147)	5,124	107,599
11	15	107,599	5.00%		(8,147)	5,787	121,534
12	16	121,534	5.00%		(8,147)	6,484	136,165
13	17	136,165	5.00%		(8,147)	7,216	151,528
14	18	151,528	5.00%		(8,147)	7,984	167,659
15	19	167,659	5.00%	(49,498)	(8,147)	6,315	132,623
16	20	132,623	5.00%	(51,973)	(8,147)	4,440	93,237
17	21	93,237	5.00%	(54,572)	(8,147)	2,341	49,153
18	22	49,153	5.00%	(57,301)	(8,147)	0	0
Totals			5.00%	(213,344)	(146,651)	66,693	0

To really drive this point home, the opportunity cost for the family during their later years is really where the price is paid.

If you saved $8,147 a year for 18 years and then let it grow past that point until your future retirement, your balance at the end of 35 years would be $551,602.

Year	Beg. of Year Acct. Value	Earnings Rate	Annual Savings	Interest Earnings	End of Year Acct. Value
1	0	5.00%	8,147	407	8,555
2	8,555	5.00%	8,147	835	17,537
3	17,537	5.00%	8,147	1,284	26,968
4	26,968	5.00%	8,147	1,756	36,872
5	36,872	5.00%	8,147	2,251	47,270
6	47,270	5.00%	8,147	2,771	58,188
7	58,188	5.00%	8,147	3,317	69,652
8	69,652	5.00%	8,147	3,890	81,689
9	81,689	5.00%	8,147	4,492	94,328
10	94,328	5.00%	8,147	5,124	107,599
11	107,599	5.00%	8,147	5,787	121,534
12	121,534	5.00%	8,147	6,484	136,165
13	136,165	5.00%	8,147	7,216	151,528
14	151,528	5.00%	8,147	7,984	167,659
15	167,659	5.00%	8,147	8,790	184,597
16	184,597	5.00%	8,147	9,637	202,381
17	202,381	5.00%	8,147	10,526	221,055
18	221,055	5.00%	8,147	11,460	240,662
19	240,662	5.00%		12,033	252,695
20	252,695	5.00%		12,635	265,330
21	265,330	5.00%		13,266	278,596
22	278,596	5.00%		13,930	292,526
23	292,526	5.00%		14,626	307,152
24	307,152	5.00%		15,358	322,510
25	322,510	5.00%		16,126	338,636
26	338,636	5.00%		16,932	355,567
27	355,567	5.00%		17,778	373,346
28	373,346	5.00%		18,667	392,013
29	392,013	5.00%		19,601	411,614
30	411,614	5.00%		20,581	432,194
31	432,194	5.00%		21,610	453,804
32	453,804	5.00%		22,690	476,494
33	476,494	5.00%		23,825	500,319
34	500,319	5.00%		25,016	525,335
35	525,335	5.00%		26,267	551,602
Totals		5.00%	(146,651)	404,951	551,602

If you spent that down through a 20-year retirement, the cash flow would be $42,154.24 per year, for a total lost opportunity cost of: $843,084.80.

Present Value:	551,602
Future Value:	0.00
Annual Int. Rate:	5.00%
Years:	20
Retirement Inc.:	(42,154.24)

A MORE CERTAIN FUTURE

The opportunity cost that comes with following the typical college path doesn't simply disappear if funded through a WMA—it gives you more options.

You're trying to prepare for something in the future that may not happen the way you think or may not happen at all. Consider the opportunity cost of that money—what that money could do between now and the time your child goes to college.

When I learned about what I do today, I cancelled the 529 plans I had and opened Wealth Maximization Accounts on each of my kids. Today, I have multiple policies on each of them. However, the idea isn't simply to treat these as 529 comparisons. The money inside a WMA can be used now, without any restrictions. In my experience, that has been a most powerful tool to teach kids, including my own, about money.

My two oldest are at an age where they understand what money is and are starting to grasp its value, which is not in the money itself but what creates it.

Instead of saying no to things they want, I can say yes. The money is borrowed against their policies, however, so it becomes their responsibility to pay it back. We call it our family bank.

My daughter Meghan has used her policies to buy numerous types of electronics and a $400 gymnastics mat, amounting to thousands of dollars cumulatively. She had to create a payback plan before she was given the money. She felt she could earn enough for the payments by increasing the amount of babysitting she did in the neighborhood. She also researched ways to earn bigger tips by giving better service, such as making little videos of the kids, making sure the house was cleaner than when the parents left, and leaving a handwritten note. This experience has given Meghan an appreciation for where money comes from, what a loan is, and what interest is—both the interest you pay and the interest you earn. I know that will benefit her in the future.

OPENING A WMA ON CHILDREN

Setting up insurance plans on your kids is even easier than setting them up on yourself. However, some companies won't let you take a policy on your child unless you already have insurance on yourself. Also, most companies have a restriction on how much you can contribute to a child's plan compared to your own coverage. It's usually 50 percent of what you have on yourself. So if you have a million dollars on yourself, the most you can get on a child is half a million dollars in insurance coverage.

You decide how much you want to contribute each month. You could start with just $50 or $100 a month. When you start, you as the parent are the policyowner. You contribute to it, you're on the hook for it, and you're the only one who can borrow against it. Once the child turns 18, however, you can create joint ownership of the policy. The child owns part of it.

For grandparents, life insurance is one of the most amazing financial gifts you can give your kids and grandkids. You own it, but it's for the benefit of your child or your grandchild.

Alternatively, as part of your estate planning, you can put the policies into a trust. This creates what's called a *waterfall effect*. It goes like this: I have policies on my parents. When they pass away, the death benefits will go into the trust they've set up for me. That money will be used to pay premiums on life insurance for me and my wife. When we pass, the money will go back into the trust, and it will be used by the kids to pay premiums. When my kids pass, the death benefit money will go into the trust for the benefit of their kids.

Of course, the cash value from the policies will be available to each generation to use as they wish.

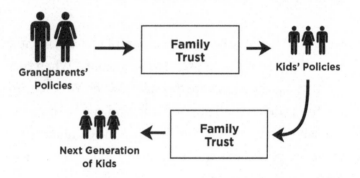

BEING ACCOUNTABLE

The "and" asset identity that your Wealth Maximization Account has is powerful, but to be successful, it requires discipline and strategy.

The loan provision and its corresponding flexibility can be a double-edged sword because of how flexible it is.

When you purchase a property or put money into a business, doing it through a policy loan keeps you accountable to replace the investment principal. To help clients understand this, we teach them about an accounting concept called Economic Value Added (EVA).[85]

This concept is used by big corporations to value the opportunity cost of big investments. They account for the opportunity cost by factoring interest on what could have been earned if they put the money somewhere else instead.

The Economic Value Added concept applies in theory at the individual level also. If you borrow against your policy, you pay interest for the use of that capital. The interest goes to the insurance company—the EVA is baked in.

You then create your own payback schedule on the same terms a bank would have required. If your purchase is a car, for instance, the interest rate would be lower, and the term would be anywhere from three to five years. If you loaned money to your business, again, the terms that a bank would require are the terms you set up for yourself. This is the best way to stay true to the strategy and ensure that you reign in the human tendencies around money.

---

85   https://www.investopedia.com/terms/e/eva.asp; https://corporatefinanceinstitute.com/resources/knowledge/valuation/economic-value-added-eva/

KEY TAKEAWAYS

- Your Wealth Maximization Account keeps your money safe and quickly accessible.

- You can borrow from your insurance company against the cash value of your policies to jump on investment opportunities.

- Wealth Maximization Accounts for your kids are the ideal way to teach them about money and also to prepare for their future purchases, such as a car, college, and beyond. Properly structured plans are a superior alternative to a 529 college savings plan.

- You can build multigenerational wealth with death benefits that cascade down to your children and grandchildren.

Your Wealth Maximization Accounts—insurance policies designed to build your personal wealth—can also be used to grow your business, as you'll learn in the next chapter.

CHAPTER 11

START, BUILD, AND PROSPER YOUR BUSINESS

"From my very first day as an entrepreneur, I've felt the only mission worth pursuing in business is to make people's lives better."

—RICHARD BRANSON

I love business. There's nothing better than being part of an idea coming to fruition through strategy, marketing, teamwork, and a collective drive to make a difference. It's a rush. Our modern society of constant evolution and change presents both incredible opportunities and major disruption of the old ways of doing things.

usiness owner or thinking of becoming a
ner, this chapter addresses ways to incorpo-
ffective structure in how you capitalize your
ncentivize your team, and ensure the proper
distance between your personal finances and those of
your business.

Head over to your complimentary copy of *The Financial
Strategy Study Guide* at headsortailsiwin.com/StudyGuide,
and there you will find several pages of commentary on
business and entrepreneurship that you may find valuable.

CAPITALIZE A BUSINESS

A new or existing business can be capitalized in many
ways. Using a policy loan is just one approach, but the
flexibility of payback and ease of borrowing makes it one
of the best ways to add capital to a company.

Entrepreneur, college professor, and author Mike Moyer
wrote a book called *Slicing Pie: Fund Your Company Without Funds,* which describes how to use capital injection to
contribute money to a new or existing business.

Capital injection can be in the form of cash, either as an
equity or capital contribution, or as a loan to the business. If you make a capital contribution, now you have
money in the bank account and you're meeting payroll

and overhead. Newer companies often lose money in the start-up phase and require this type of ongoing capital support. The question becomes, *when do you start getting that money back?*

Most business owners don't have a uniform answer for that. They end up taking the money in a random and uncalculated way, which often puts a constraint on the business's finances.

When there are multiple partners involved, the situation becomes even more complicated and disjointed. Who gets how much? When? How do you decide? Moyer explains some good solutions to this, using what he calls dynamic equity splitting.

Additionally, you can circumvent the dilemma altogether by personally lending money to the business. It's what I typically do with my business interests and what we teach our business owner clients to do.

Here's how it works:

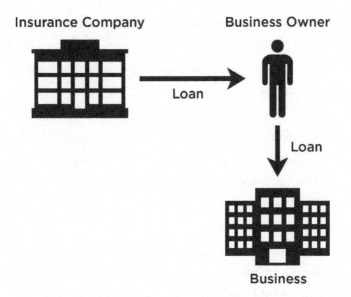

Insurance Company

Loan

Business Owner

Loan

Business

1. You request a loan from your insurance company and deposit the funds into your personal bank account.
2. You then make a formal loan to the company in question, documented by a promissory note and amortization schedule. These are recorded on the business balance sheet and in your corporate minutes.
3. The loan has a specified interest rate, one that is comparable to the terms of outside financing by a bank.
4. The terms of the loan can vary. Common arrangements are a fully amortized payback, or a line of credit, where the repayment is of interest only. A rule of thumb is to model your loan after the terms and interest rate a traditional bank would give you.

Once the company starts making money and turns a profit,

the next goal is typically to pay off debts. That means paying off the loan you made to the company. If you made a capital contribution instead, that shows up as company equity and the sense of urgency when it comes to repaying a capital contribution isn't equal.

Capitalizing your business this way aligns with the business practice called Economic Value Added (EVA) mentioned earlier. EVA is used by companies such as Coca-Cola, Best Buy, Mary Kay, and Whole Foods to assess the cost of capital associated with new ventures.[86] The measurement accounts for the lost opportunity cost of the money used to provide capital to a new location or venture.

Whole Foods states that, "EVA is a guiding philosophy for investing the company's resources."[87] It states that its cost of capital is 8 percent and each new location has the goal of achieving profitability beyond this 8 percent measurement within five years.

Most business owners aren't at the Whole Foods level, and an 8 percent benchmark may not be suitable for your respective business. But modeling their business practice

---

86 http://fortune.com/2013/05/06/eva-stars-of-the-fortune-500/; https://www.cluteinstitute.com/ojs/index.php/JABR/article/download/2112/2089/

87 https://www.investopedia.com/stock-analysis/061515/5-things-whole-foods-management-wants-you-know-wfm.aspx

of valuing the cost of capital is a wise method to ensure your own success and the success of the business.

THE CASH, RESERVES, AND LIQUIDITY DILEMMA

In my experience, business owners tend to keep a lot of cash in their business. That's understandable. However, a lot of cash could be a risky proposition from a liability standpoint.

If your business is ever sued, that money can be in jeopardy. Additionally, keeping that cash in a bank triggers a large opportunity cost. Business bank accounts pay similar returns as personal bank accounts. The lost interest you might earn from your Wealth Maximization Account can be significant over time.

To avoid carrying too much cash, you can use your established Wealth Maximization Account to carve out profits from your capital account. The profits can be held outside of the business in a creditor-protected private asset. It becomes your personal savings, your liquid wealth, and provides an ideal separation of your personal assets and business assets.

Most business structures are taxed as pass-through entities—either a partnership or an S corporation. This means that the profits are taxed at the personal income tax level.

From a tax perspective, it doesn't matter whether you keep the money in the business or take a personal distribution—you are taxed equally.

The following side-by-side comparison shows how large that opportunity cost can be over time.

Assumptions for a business savings account:

· Annual business cash flow: $100,000
· Business savings account APY: 0.5 percent
· Marginal tax bracket: 33 percent
· Years to analyze: 20

Year	Beg. of Year Acct. Value	Earnings Rate	Annual Cash Flow	Interest Earnings	Taxes	End of Year Acct. Value
1	100,000	0.50%	100,000	500	(165)	100,335
2	100,335	0.50%	100,000	1,002	(331)	201,006
3	201,006	0.50%	100,000	1,505	(497)	302,014
4	302,014	0.50%	100,000	2,010	(663)	403,361
5	403,361	0.50%	100,000	2,517	(831)	505,048
6	505,048	0.50%	100,000	3,025	(998)	607,074
7	607,074	0.50%	100,000	3,535	(1,167)	709,443
8	709,443	0.50%	100,000	4,047	(1,336)	812,155
9	812,155	0.50%	100,000	4,561	(1,505)	915,210
10	915,210	0.50%	100,000	5,076	(1,675)	1,018,611
11	1,018,611	0.50%	100,000	5,593	(1,846)	1,122,359
12	1,122,359	0.50%	100,000	6,112	(2,017)	1,226,454
13	1,226,454	0.50%	100,000	6,632	(2,189)	1,330,897
14	1,330,897	0.50%	100,000	7,154	(2,361)	1,435,691
15	1,435,691	0.50%	100,000	7,678	(2,534)	1,540,835
16	1,540,835	0.50%	100,000	8,204	(2,707)	1,646,332
17	1,646,332	0.50%	100,000	8,731	(2,881)	1,752,182
18	1,752,182	0.50%	100,000	9,261	(3,056)	1,858,387
19	1,858,387	0.50%	100,000	9,792	(3,231)	1,964,948
20	1,964,948	0.50%	100,000	10,325	(3,407)	2,071,865
Totals		0.50%	2,000,000	107,262	(35,396)	2,071,865

Results:

- Total contributions: $2,000,000
- Interest earned: $71,865
- Taxes Paid: $35,396
- Ending balance: $2,071,865

Assumptions for an established[88] Wealth Maximization Account:

- Annual business cash flow: $100,000
- Interest and dividend paid on cash value: 5 percent
- Years to analyze: 20

Year	Beg. of Year Acct. Value	Earnings Rate	Annual Cash Flow	Interest Earnings	End of Year Acct. Value
1	100,000	5.00%	100,000	5,000	105,000
2	105,000	5.00%	100,000	10,250	215,250
3	215,250	5.00%	100,000	15,763	331,013
4	331,013	5.00%	100,000	21,551	452,563
5	452,563	5.00%	100,000	27,628	580,191
6	580,191	5.00%	100,000	34,010	714,201
7	714,201	5.00%	100,000	40,710	854,911
8	854,911	5.00%	100,000	47,746	1,002,656
9	1,002,656	5.00%	100,000	55,133	1,157,789
10	1,157,789	5.00%	100,000	62,889	1,320,679
11	1,320,679	5.00%	100,000	71,034	1,491,713
12	1,491,713	5.00%	100,000	79,586	1,671,298
13	1,671,298	5.00%	100,000	88,565	1,859,863
14	1,859,863	5.00%	100,000	97,993	2,057,856
15	2,057,856	5.00%	100,000	107,893	2,265,749
16	2,265,749	5.00%	100,000	118,287	2,484,037
17	2,484,037	5.00%	100,000	129,202	2,713,238
18	2,713,238	5.00%	100,000	140,662	2,953,900
19	2,953,900	5.00%	100,000	152,695	3,206,595
20	3,206,595	5.00%	100,000	165,330	3,471,925
Totals		5.00%	2,000,000	1,471,925	3,471,925

---

88 A policy or multiple policies that have been set up before allocating business reserves.

Results:

- Total contributions: $2,000,000
- Interest earned: $1,471,925
- Taxes Paid: $0
- Ending balance: $3,471,925

A business saving $100,000 at a traditional bank over the course of 20 years equates to more than $1.4 million in opportunity cost.

I keep a few months of cash reserve in my business, but I keep everything else inside multiple WMAs. That way, if my business ever needs money—for, say, a marketing campaign, software, a new employee, or a new venture—I can use the liquidity of a policy loan to provide the capital. Also, the earnings are multiple-times greater than the typical depository account.

Common business purchases using your Wealth Maximization Account might include:

- Equipment
- Software
- Marketing campaign
- New employee
- Office build-out
- Furniture
- Quarterly income tax payments

- Business merger and acquisition
- Stock buy-back or partner buy-out
- Business vehicles
- Inventory financing

HOW TO INCENTIVIZE YOUR EMPLOYEES

As an employer, you want to create a positive workplace that inspires your employees and keeps them happy to work for you. The expectation today is a benefits package that includes an employer-sponsored, 401(k) retirement plan that employees can contribute to.

The attraction is that, when times are good, the employer makes a matching contribution. I discussed in detail the downsides of these types of plans, especially as they pertain to you as the business owner, in Chapter Four.

To recap:

- The plans are expensive to set up and administer.
- As the owner, your contributions to the plan tie up money that can't be used for the business.
- The employer contribution means restrictions to rewarding specific employees without having to reward others.
- 401(k) plans are portable and aren't usually a reason to stay with an employer if a better opportunity arises elsewhere.

- Although there is little or no liability for money lost inside of plans, when money is lost in a market decline, employee morale is likely to be affected.

Fortunately, there are other ways to incentivize employees.

SECTION 162 PLANS

In Chapter Four, I discussed in detail why the 401(k) plan was never meant to be a retirement plan. For years, it was never used—in fact, it was almost repealed a few times. Then Ted Benna figured out a way to use it today and 401(k) plans became the predominant employer-sponsored retirement vehicle they are today.

Among the thousands of pages of tax code is Section 162, another little-known provision. Section 162 provides another way employers can incentivize their team without the restrictions of a 401(k).

As an employer, you can provide compensation to employees by offering them a Section 162 bonus plan. These plans can be used to fund an employee-owned insurance policy designed to be a Wealth Maximization Account. Section 162 plans are very flexible and surprisingly simple to set up.

In a 162 plan, the business agrees to pay all or part of the premiums, including the Paid-Up Additions (PUA) rider, which is owned by the employee. The employee gets all the benefits and protections of the policy and gets to keep the cash value that builds up in it. The advantage to the employer is that the bonus amount you put into the policy is fully tax-deductible as reasonable compensation. It's not tax-deferred to the employee, but the plan can be designed in such a way that the after-tax cost to them is reduced or even eliminated. Additional advantages of the 162 plan include:

- Vesting schedules set by the employer if an employee leaves early in their career
- No IRS approval
- Unequal compensation among employees

The following diagram demonstrates how the 162 plan works.

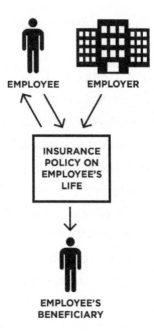

EMPLOYEE   EMPLOYER

INSURANCE
POLICY ON
EMPLOYEE'S
LIFE

EMPLOYEE'S
BENEFICIARY

1. The selected employee applies for and owns a life insurance policy on his or her own life.

2. Under the terms of a written agreement, the employer pays the annual premiums either directly or by way of a cash bonus. These payments are deductible (as long as the amounts are reasonable) and are considered additional compensation to the employee.

3. The employee can access the policy's cash value on an income-tax-free basis through loans and withdrawals. The employer may restrict the access if desired.

4. At death, the employee's named beneficiary receives the proceeds. The death benefit is free of federal income tax.

NONQUALIFIED DEFERRED COMPENSATION PLANS

Nonqualified deferred compensation plans (NQDCs), also called IRS Section 409A plans, are agreements between you and an employee (typically an executive) to defer part of the employee's annual compensation until a future date. That date could be in five years or in 10 years, or it could be when the employee retires. The deferred income isn't taxed until the employee actually receives it in the future. In the meantime, as the employer, you need to find a safe and profitable way to invest the deferred compensation the employee has entrusted to you. The ideal way to fund a NQDC plan is using a Wealth Maximization Account, owned by the employer, and for the benefit of the employee at a future date.

NQDC plans are less complex from the employer's perspective. They're flexible, inexpensive to set up, and they don't need to be approved by the IRS or other government agencies. They're a great way to retain key employees and are often called "golden handcuffs." Additionally, they help the company's cash flow, because you don't have to pay the deferred compensation until sometime in the future.

The following diagram demonstrates how the plan works.

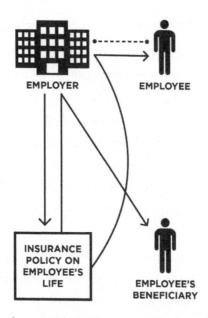

EMPLOYER   EMPLOYEE

INSURANCE
POLICY ON
EMPLOYEE'S
LIFE

EMPLOYEE'S
BENEFICIARY

1. The employer and employee enter into an agreement specifying future compensation. This future income is currently taxed if the employer funds the agreement.

2. The employer purchases an insurance policy on the employee's life. This unofficial funding method ensures tax deferral on the future income.

3. When the employee retires (or otherwise meets the conditions of the agreement), the employer begins to pay the benefits using the policy's cash value. These benefits are subject to the tax rules regarding policy withdrawals, loans, and surrenders.

4. At the employee's death, the employer pays out the death benefit to the employee's named beneficiary. To avoid taxation of these death benefits, the employer must meet the notice and consent requirement.

THE 412(E)(3): A FULLY INSURED PENSION

The fully insured pension is a defined benefit plan, guaranteed by an insurance company, not the underlying business. It specifies a future income stream for an employee, usually executives, owners, or stakeholders. After an employee has been with the company for a specified time (becomes vested), they receive a predetermined benefit from the employer for the rest of their lives. There might also be a survivor benefit for a spouse.

During the 1980s and 1990s, pensions lost their appeal due to regulatory and compliance burdens in conjunction with increased liability to the company. This environment gave rise to the 401(k).

However, Section 412(e)(3) plans are exempt from the complexities of those pension rules and are not the company's liability. The liability is guaranteed by the insurance company.

These plans allow for large contributions and are attractive to a smaller company's owner or partner and highly paid employees. They're helpful for retaining these top performers.

PROTECTING YOUR BUSINESS

I am passionate about business. I believe you are the

number one asset; the business is second. Many of our clients are business owners who want to maximize their capital, grow their business, and protect their assets. My team and I teach about the various roles that a Wealth Maximization Account plays in the business setting and the corresponding personal financial situation. Here are a few key concepts that are part of a solid business foundation.

KEY PERSON INSURANCE

Key person insurance is life insurance taken out by the employer on employees who are crucial to the ongoing success of the company. If a key employee dies, the business could be in real trouble. Life insurance helps bridge the gap. In a small business, the key employees are owners, founders, partners—if these people unexpectedly pass, the company could die with them. Key person insurance can keep the company going through the loss. In a larger business, the key employees are also high-level executives, top salespeople, and other essential employees. Let's say you have a key person like a C-level or VP-level person that took two years to hire. If that person dies, it could take two years to replace them (not to mention time to get them trained up), so the opportunity cost is huge. You can protect yourself against that with a properly designed key person insurance policy. This insurance can be term instead of permanent and convertible to a Wealth Maximization Account in the future.

BUY-SELL AND STOCK BUY-BACK FUNDING

If you have partners in your business, buy-sell or stock redemption agreements can help smooth the transition and keep the business going if a partner dies. A buy-sell agreement is a legal agreement that gives the other partners or owners the ability to buy out the estate of that individual at a certain price if one partner dies. If there's no agreement in place, if someone dies, suddenly the estate of that person is your new partner. The ideal way to fund these agreements is partially or wholly through life insurance.

TWO ADVANCED INSURANCE FUNDING PROGRAMS

The strategies mentioned above are protection measures taken in advance of unexpected events. The proceeding strategies are advanced concepts for higher net worth individuals, families, and businesses.

Premium-Financed Insurance

Recently, a new approach has become available to bigger business owners who are purchasing new insurance or already have similar policies in place. They can obtain premium-financed insurance, which significantly reduces the cost. If the business is big enough, banks will lend you the money to pay your premiums on very, very favorable terms. You only have to pay the interest on the premium loan, which means you could obtain permanent coverage at a term insurance price.

Premium-financed insurance is an advanced strategy and not for everyone. Banks that participate in these programs require participants to meet certain requirements. If you do meet these criteria, this is one of the best financial decisions the owner of a bigger business can make regarding their foundational levels of protection.

The Split-Dollar Arrangement

How does Michigan head coach Jim Harbaugh make $2 million a year and pay less than 1 percent in income tax? He uses a split-dollar arrangement.

Split-dollar arrangements aren't a new concept. They're often used to attract and retain valuable employees. The arrangement is structured to fund a large life insurance plan on an employee. The economic benefit (death benefit) is split with the employee's estate when he or she passes away.

In the Harbaugh case, the University of Michigan entered into an arrangement as part of his compensation package. They loaned him two million a year for six years for the purchase of a large life insurance policy. Harbaugh is responsible for claiming the amount of interest from the loan as earned income on his income taxes. The interest rate used in these transactions is called the Long-Term Applicable Federal Interest Rate, set by the federal government. Here's how the benefit package pencils out:

- $2 million of compensation to purchase life insurance that Coach Harbaugh owns
- Cash value, which Harbaugh can use, grows tax-free
- A 2.24 percent interest rate was used for the first year of the arrangement, which means Harbaugh had to claim $44,800 of income on his tax return

If Harbaugh had been in the 39.6 percent tax bracket when the arrangement started, his tax liability would be $17,740 or 0.8 percent of the $2,000,000. Split-dollar plans are typically used as part of a comprehensive benefits package negotiation between a key person and their employer. In the appropriate situation, these plans provide lucrative benefits to the employee. However, it also benefits the employer with a committed employee and an economic reimbursement in the future.

The following diagram shows how the split dollar arrangement works.

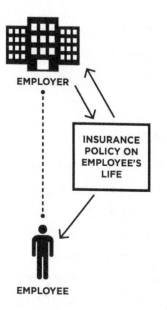

EMPLOYER

INSURANCE POLICY ON EMPLOYEE'S LIFE

EMPLOYEE

1. An employer who wants to offer a fringe benefit to a key employee enters into a formal agreement to split the costs and benefits of a permanent life insurance policy.

2. The employee purchases the policy and then collaterally assigns it to the employer.

3. The employer pays all premiums, which are treated as a series of interest-bearing loans. If the employer chooses to forgive the loan interest each year, the employee includes the amount of the forgiven interest in the gross income and pays taxes on that amount.

4. At the employee's death (or the termination of the agreement), the employer recovers its total premiums or the cash value, depending on the terms of the agreement.

5. The balance of the policy value is distributed to the employee or paid as death proceeds to the employee's beneficiary.

KEY TAKEAWAYS

- As a business owner, you have many ways to use The Perpetual Wealth Strategy to grow, build, prosper, and protect your company.
- The Wealth Maximization Account is an ideal funding source to capitalize a business.
- You can offer a few incentive plans to your employees through plans other than a 401(k).
- Life insurance protects your business through key person insurance, buy-sell, and stock redemption agreements.

There are numerous ways to use The Perpetual Wealth Strategy to improve the productivity, incentives, and long-term well-being of your employees and your business.

But what about you?

Let's take the next chapter to discuss how you can ideally prepare for your financial future.

CHAPTER 12

===

YOUR FINANCIAL FUTURE

"There is no passion to be found playing small—in settling for a life that is less than the one you are capable of living."

—NELSON MANDELA

I fundamentally disagree with the idea of retirement. It's anti-life and inherently flawed. The goal of The Perpetual Wealth Strategy isn't retirement at 65. It's financial freedom as soon as possible.

A good financial strategy isn't to stop producing but to structure your finances, investments, and employment to make the biggest difference and achieve a fulfilling lifestyle. The preparation for this lifestyle is just as much mental as it is financial, which in turn fosters a paradigm shift.

Your heart turns from maxing out your 401(k) contributions, suffering through unhealthy office culture, and sacrificing time and energy away from your family. Instead, your goals become establishing liquidity, investing in yourself (your greatest asset to maximize your earning potential), investing in assets for maximum cash flow, and then discovering your calling, unique genius, and a conducive professional environment to execute that discovery.

That environment will provide flexibility to mix in the other important aspects of life, such as family events and travel. Imagine a lifestyle where your investments pay you cash flow monthly and you use your years of training, experience, and wisdom to consult, work remotely, or be with a company that offers flexible lifestyle benefits. Today, more than ever, that lifestyle is absolutely possible.

Many live it every day.

NATHAN AND ELIZA'S STORY

The technology industry is one of the most competitive, fast-paced, and demanding environments out there. Nathan and Eliza were married not only to each other but their careers as well. Both were executives for Fortune 500 technology giants. They were paid well and established a healthy financial statement, which was set up to let them retire in 10 to 15 years. However, after two decades of saving, they began to realize the flaw in retirement and knew there had to be another way.

STEP 1: YOU ARE YOUR GREATEST ASSET

Their first move was pursuing education to learn about other ways to invest besides the typical financial plan. They began listening to investment podcasts and attending live events. They took vacation time and attended several personal development and leadership conferences, as well as mastermind groups. These steps made them realize the lack of control they had with their assets. They also realized that they possessed professional attributes that were valuable in other aspects.

STEP 2: FINANCIAL STRATEGY

They ceased their retirement contributions and instead shifted assets and ongoing savings to Wealth Maximization Accounts. They borrowed against their accumulating cash value and purchased several investment properties. They invested in partnerships that acquired new and existing apartment complexes.

STEP 3: PURSUE YOUR PASSIONS AND MAKE MONEY DOING IT

Nathan grew up with a passion for role-playing games such

as Dungeons and Dragons. This genre of the gaming world is popular in the United States and internationally. Interest overseas is growing at a rapid pace. During his period of awakening, an opportunity arose for Nathan to acquire one of the primary companies in this space, including the intellectual property rights and the distribution network. Nathan's ability to effectively manage teams and projects gave him the experience and capacity to form a team to acquire, normalize, and grow the already successful company. He is now the primary shareholder and executive in a company and industry he loves.

During her lengthy career, Eliza prided herself in mentoring countless individuals at each of the companies she worked for. She taught them to navigate the fast-paced tech world and life at a Fortune 500 company. She loves to teach and mentor. Eliza also discovered another set of assets. Her experience running budgets north of a billion dollars and managing teams consisting of several hundred employees was valuable to the outside world. She was approached by former colleagues and acquaintances with opportunities to consult for start-ups and private equity firms who were performing due diligence on companies they wanted to acquire. Her expertise in business operations, proper team structure, budget and financial management, and effective strategic planning was crucial to ensure that, with additional capital, the growth of these potential acquisitions would take place.

STEP 4: THE FINANCIAL FREEDOM LIFESTYLE

Financial freedom isn't playing two rounds of golf, watching daytime TV, and playing bridge. Financial freedom is having a choice of how to spend your time and energy, where money isn't the primary factor in the decision. Financial freedom is a strategy. If your aim reroutes from the idea of retirement to the idea of financial freedom, you can achieve it much sooner and with less money than you think.

GAMING YOUR RETIREMENT YEARS

Over the years, it has been extremely difficult for me to work with older clients. I have to tell them the truth about the idea of retirement and why their finances won't allow for the future they hoped for.

Too many of these clients are relying on a combination of their Social Security benefits and distribution from their 401(k) accounts to fund their retirement. I've run scenarios over and over—it's mathematically not possible to pull it off, given the state of the economy and society.

First, let's identify the sobering state of what typical financial advice has convinced the American public to expect.

TYPICAL FINANCIAL ADVICE: *GROWTH*

Let's assume you save 10 percent of your earned income for 30 years. (Hardly anyone does this—the actual average of the personal savings rate since 1988 is 5.6 percent.[89]) You can expect to live another 30 years beyond that. When you factor in market volatility, inflation, and the likelihood of major Social Security and Medicare reform, the math doesn't work. There isn't enough money to make this possible.

The calculations are sobering and not being discussed in the typical financial planning world. In 1988, the median income was just shy of $20,000 per year.[90] If we assume a savings rate of 10 percent or $2,000, and increase the contribution by 2.56 percent per year, which is the CPI (Consumer Price Index) rate for the period of 1988 to 2017, this is what your ending balance would be if you invested in the S&P 500 without any fees: $283,475—and remember, fewer than 20 percent of money managers ever beat the S&P.

---

89   https://fred.stlouisfed.org/data/PSAVERT.txt

90   https://en.wikipedia.org/wiki/Average_Indexed_Monthly_Earnings

Year	Beg. of Year Acct. Value	Earnings Rate	Annual Savings	Interest Earnings	End of Year Acct. Value
1988		12.40%	2,000	248	2,248
1989	2,248	27.25%	2,051	1,172	5,471
1990	5,471	(6.56%)	2,104	(497)	7,078
1991	7,078	26.30%	2,158	2,429	11,664
1992	11,664	4.46%	2,213	620	14,497
1993	14,497	7.06%	2,269	1,183	17,949
1994	17,949	(1.54%)	2,328	(312)	19,965
1995	19,965	34.11%	2,387	7,624	29,976
1996	29,976	20.26%	2,448	6,570	38,995
1997	38,995	31.01%	2,511	12,870	54,376
1998	54,376	26.69%	2,575	15,197	72,148
1999	72,148	19.51%	2,641	14,592	89,381
2000	89,381	(10.14%)	2,709	(9,337)	82,753
2001	82,753	(13.04%)	2,778	(11,153)	74,378
2002	74,378	(23.37%)	2,849	(18,047)	59,180
2003	59,180	26.38%	2,922	16,383	78,485
2004	78,485	8.99%	2,997	7,328	88,810
2005	88,810	3.00%	3,074	2,757	94,641
2006	94,641	13.62%	3,152	13,319	111,112
2007	111,112	3.53%	3,233	4,036	118,381
2008	118,381	(38.49%)	3,316	(46,836)	74,861
2009	74,861	23.45%	3,401	18,356	96,617
2010	96,617	12.78%	3,488	12,796	112,901
2011	112,901	(0.00%)	3,577	(4)	116,475
2012	116,475	13.41%	3,669	16,106	136,249
2013	136,249	29.60%	3,763	41,445	181,457
2014	181,457	11.39%	3,859	21,109	206,425
2015	206,425	(0.73%)	3,958	(1,529)	208,854
2016	208,854	9.54%	4,059	20,301	233,214
2017	233,214	19.42%	4,163	46,098	283,475
Totals		9.68%	88,650	194,825	283,475

TYPICAL FINANCIAL ADVICE: *INCOME*

The rule of thumb for determining the income distribution of portfolio-based assets is known as a Monte Carlo simulation, informally referred to as the 4 percent rule. The rule provides the investor with a percentage of the portfolio they can withdraw from their account. The rule is established based on the number of retirement years and the probability of *not* running out of money. *Not running out of money* means a positive portfolio balance—that you would be left with at least one dollar. So, for a portfolio starting out at $1 million, following the 4 percent rule, the maximum annual income would be $40,000.

Here is a chart that helps illustrate the concept:[91]

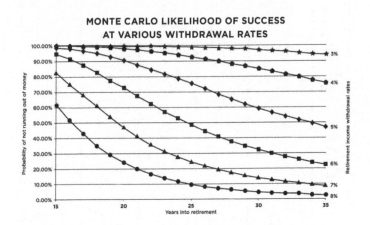

MONTE CARLO LIKELIHOOD OF SUCCESS AT VARIOUS WITHDRAWAL RATES

Wade Pfau, a Certified Financial Analyst at Retiremen-tresearcher.com, has written extensively about the current market environment and why the 4 percent rule no longer applies. Pfau concludes that 4 percent is much too aggres-

---

91   This graphical depiction is for illustrative purposes only. The illustration was derived using market data reported in the 2018 SBBI Yearbook by Roger Ibbotson – additional information can be found at www.headsortailsiwin.com/studyguide. These simulations have been run using a 50/25/25 portfolio of S&P Total Return Index/USA Government Bond Series/Corporate Bond Series with the respective time frame of 1926-2017. Additionally, a portfolio expense of 1.5% and inflation rate of 3% was assessed in the assumptions. The projections regarding the likelihood of investment outcomes are hypothetical and may not be used to predict or project investment results – an investment cannot be made directly into an index. Past performance is no guarantee of future results.

sive and that a better starting place would be 3 percent. (For a video and e-book by Pfau that explains why market volatility keeps the distribution percentage so low, head over to headsortailsiwin.com/StudyGuide.)

Let's return to the example highlighted in *Growth*. If you began saving 10 percent of your income beginning in 1988 and earned the same return as the S&P 500 without fees, your portfolio balance would be $283,475. Using the Monte Carlo income distribution rate for 30 years at the recommended 3 percent gives you a retirement income of $8,504 a year, or $708 per month. If you increased your savings contributions by 5 percent per year, your portfolio balance would be $376,911 and your distribution would be $11,307 a year, or $942 per month.

It doesn't work!

If you want to analyze your personal numbers through this exercise, there is a calculator in the online study guide that you have access to, *The Financial Strategy Study Guide*. Go check it out: headsortailsiwin.com/StudyGuide.

To compound the retirement dilemma, Social Security is a mess. According to their 2015 audit, the trust fund will be completely depleted in 2034. Betting on Social Security alone for retirement is not possible, even if it does survive beyond what is projected. The average Social Security income today is $1,342 per month, hardly a livable wage.[92]

Based on the typical logic of financial planners these days, here's how the numbers would have to look:

Let's assume a savings period of 30 years, at 50 percent a year—yes, half their annual earned income—increasing by 5 percent a year. The money is in an S&P 500 fund with management fees of 1.5 percent.

Year	Beg. of Year Acct. Value	Earnings Rate	Annual Savings	Interest Earnings	Taxes	End of Year Acct. Value
1988		12.40%	10,000	1,240	(169)	11,071
1989	11,071	27.25%	10,500	5,878	(412)	27,038
1990	27,038	(6.56%)	11,025	(2,495)	(534)	35,034
1991	35,034	26.30%	11,576	12,260	(883)	57,986
1992	57,986	4.46%	12,155	3,131	(1,099)	72,174
1993	72,174	7.06%	12,763	5,992	(1,364)	89,565
1994	89,565	(1.54%)	13,401	(1,585)	(1,521)	99,860
1995	99,860	34.11%	14,071	38,863	(2,292)	150,502
1996	150,502	20.26%	14,775	33,491	(2,982)	195,786
1997	195,786	31.01%	15,513	65,520	(4,152)	272,667
1998	272,667	26.69%	16,289	77,108	(5,491)	360,574
1999	360,574	19.51%	17,103	73,687	(6,770)	444,593
2000	444,593	(10.14%)	17,959	(46,899)	(6,235)	409,418
2001	409,418	(13.04%)	18,856	(55,846)	(5,586)	366,842
2002	366,842	(23.37%)	19,799	(90,353)	(4,444)	291,844
2003	291,844	26.38%	20,789	82,474	(5,927)	389,181
2004	389,181	8.99%	21,829	36,964	(6,720)	441,254
2005	441,254	3.00%	22,920	13,930	(7,172)	470,933
2006	470,933	13.62%	24,066	67,416	(8,436)	553,979
2007	553,979	3.53%	25,270	20,445	(8,995)	590,698
2008	590,698	(38.49%)	26,533	(237,546)	(5,695)	373,990
2009	373,990	23.45%	27,860	94,250	(7,441)	488,658
2010	488,658	12.78%	29,253	66,203	(8,762)	575,352
2011	575,352	(0.00%)	30,715	(19)	(9,091)	596,957
2012	596,957	13.41%	32,251	84,350	(10,703)	702,855
2013	702,855	29.60%	33,864	218,078	(14,322)	940,474
2014	940,474	11.39%	35,557	111,176	(16,308)	1,070,899
2015	1,070,899	(0.73%)	37,335	(8,052)	(16,503)	1,083,678
2016	1,083,678	9.54%	39,201	107,067	(18,449)	1,211,497
2017	1,211,497	19.42%	41,161	243,266	(22,439)	1,473,485
Totals		9.68%	664,388	1,019,993	(210,896)	1,473,485

92   https://www.ssa.gov/policy/docs/statcomps/supplement/2017/index.html

The numbers work out to 30 years of retirement income at the recommended 3 percent Monte Carlo rate, or $44,204 a year. Add in the average Social Security income of $16,104, and the total is $60,308, which is the median earned income for 2017.

This scenario does not include income taxes.

The idea of retirement at 65 was concocted to make way for a younger workforce. Social Security was originally developed as a contributory system for only a small percentage of the population to pay retirement benefits for those over the age of 65. In 1935, when Social Security was introduced, few people made it to that age.

Social Security is a system that doesn't work in our day and age.

The government takes 7.65 percent from you and 7.65 percent from your employer every paycheck and uses it to buy government bonds, which in turn fund the retirement benefits. By law, that's the only investment the government can make with Social Security money. The problem is that the bonds don't have any marketable value, and they pay a low return. The rate of return on these government securities only goes so far when it comes to paying benefits.

Right now, as the huge baby boomer generation retires, more money is coming out of Social Security than is going in. About 62 million Americans were getting Social Security retirement benefits in 2017.[93] By 2035, 79 million people over the age of 65 are going to be on Social Security, not counting those that are disabled or underage. Major changes will need to be made before then to be sure everyone who's been paying into the system will still receive benefits.

Relying on your 401(k) and Social Security to fund all or most of your retirement is dangerous. You won't be able to live anywhere near the way you do now.

Thankfully, there are options.

On your financial statement, the goal is maximum cash flow. On your Human Capital statement, the goal is earning maximum income by doing what you love or enjoy, which also aligns with a fulfilling lifestyle.

CONQUERING RETIREMENT ANXIETY

The top two concerns people have about their future are: [94]

- Am I going to outlive my money?

---

93 https://www.ssa.gov/oact/STATS/OASDIbenies.html

94 http://news.gallup.com/poll/210890/americans-financial-anxieties-ease-2017.aspx

- Will I have enough for my healthcare expenses?

Thinking about retirement keeps us in a state of constant anxiety. You're gambling on an uncertain future, rolling the dice on your longevity and your health. That's stressful.

To get rid of that anxiety, you must face reality. The reality is that the odds aren't in your favor. You must face how much money you have. You must face the reality that the future of Social Security is uncertain. You must face the reality that you're likely to live into your 80s or beyond, so your money has to last longer.

Understanding the reality and then figuring out your alternatives is the only way to overcome that anxiety.

You have a variety of ways to beat the system.

BEATING THE SYSTEM

Retirement and financial freedom are not the same thing. The definition of retirement is to take out of service or to stop contributing. Financial freedom is the state of mind that is achieved when money is not the primary motivator of your decisions and is achieved when you have efficiency of both your financial statement and Human Capital statement. I have a great example of how to do just that.

THE LIFE OF BRYAN

Bryan is a highly paid executive at a printing business. He's good at his job, but his industry is shifting, and the hustle isn't as enjoyable as it once was. I met Bryan when he was in his early 50s. We set up a Wealth Maximization Account and structured his estate plan. He began purchasing investment real estate as part of his overall strategy. However, over our years of meetings, he grew increasingly concerned that, even though his financial strategy was improving, his overall savings and investments wouldn't last him through his retirement years. Despite my discouragement, he was still contributing to his 401(k) because of the generous employer match. However, his funds were still recovering from the severe hit in the 2008–2009 market downturn, and the worry was that another market correction would ruin any hope of a secure financial future. His compensation also was declining due to pressure in his industry.

He hated the thought of having to work forever, stuck in a job he didn't enjoy. He also realized that his knowledge and skillset was in an industry that wouldn't be around for much longer.

We sat down again and revamped his strategy. This time, the goal was to figure out how to position his assets and produce the most amount of cash flow with the least amount of risk.

We first assessed his 401(k) and the value of the employer match. He assured me that his match was like a 100 percent return on his money. I didn't argue that the match wasn't valuable. Instead, I showed him that the long-term economic benefit of the match was much less than he supposed. It was a high return on his contribution, but certainly not the entire balance. At the time, the match was $9,000 per year, but it was only available if Bryan also contributed $9,000. His 401(k) balance was $1.2 million. The $9,000 employer match was roughly a 0.75 percent addition to his balance. (For a video that walks you through the complexities of how a 401(k) works, see my website at headsortailsiwin.com/StudyGuide.)

Bryan didn't stop contributing to his 401(k), but he pulled back to the level of getting the match, not the maximum level he was used to. We decided to open another insurance policy with some cash he had elsewhere and from the cash flow that was previously going into his 401(k).

Next, we analyzed the future portfolio income of his retirement account using the Monte Carlo simulation.

When I taught Bryan this, we were assuming that over the coming years his 401(k) balance would grow to about $1.5 million. At that level, the yearly distribution recommendation given by typical financial planners would be $45,000 to $60,000, which wasn't even close to what

Bryan was expecting. Even with his real estate cash flow and Social Security, the number still left him short.

Fortunately, Bryan had set up sufficient insurance to allow for a strategy we call the Covered Asset, which could boost income by 100 percent or more and guarantees it for life.

Currently, income rates for this type of contract are between 6 and 7 percent of the portfolio balance. Therefore, instead of succumbing to the Monte Carlo distribution amount of $45,000 to $60,000, which isn't guaranteed, he could have a guaranteed income of $90,000 to $109,000 for the rest of his life.

In addition to that boost of income, our strategy sessions included the use of proprietary software to calculate his and his wife's optimal Social Security income. The calculations included the best ages to file and looked at the provisional income thresholds that would trigger income tax on up to 85 percent of their social benefits, as well as Medicare surcharges if that retirement income is not properly managed with the help of an experienced Wealth Strategist.

Bryan's original plan was to set up a Wealth Maximization Account to grow his wealth tax-free and use policy loans to invest in real estate, fund his kid's college education, and make large personal purchases instead of using a bank.

As life went on, his financial situation evolved, and the focus was no longer on growing wealth but on securing future passive income.

Bryan had a plan for the coming years and learned how to shift the role of his assets, which included his Wealth Maximization Accounts, to secure the maximum amount of passive income in exchange for the least amount of risk.

CAREER REBIRTH

Even with all the improvement we made in his financial future, Bryan realized that he didn't really want to retire. He wanted to continue to contribute and use all the experience he'd accumulated over his career. This new mindset resulted from the knowledge that regardless of what he did, his financial future was intact.

He began looking for opportunities. He started by making a list of attributes his dream career would have. He wanted the flexibility to work part-time (only 20 hours a week), including generous vacation and time off. Bryan also started to build a list of his skills, experience, and overall business sense. He included on this list his vast professional network of other executives, business owners, and influencers he had met over the years. During the process, he discovered a handful of opportunities to take his reputation, skillset, and experience to consulting and freelancing roles.

The primary motivations for people wanting to retire is stepping away from unruly leadership, poor office culture, and unrewarding environments—not retiring from being productive, contributing, and sharing what they've learned and are passionate about.

Don't retire. Start the second phase of your professional life as an executive-level consultant or a freelancer, or simply find a business whose culture aligns with your values and drive. You can reinvent yourself or create a more flexible second career. Use your skills, your expertise, your mastery to stay on top of your game, contribute to society, and still get paid. You can design it to have the flexibility to travel, to visit kids and grandkids, or do service work. The world we live in has made this possible.

Bryan did a lot of research into best practices and approaches to these opportunities. He put together a great list of books, websites, and other resources that can be found in *The Financial Strategy Study Guide,* found at headsortailsiwin.com/StudyGuide.

INCOME STRATEGIES TO BEAT THE
TYPICAL ADVICE

STRATEGY #1: THE COVERED ASSET STRATEGY

For those who consider themselves at the tail end of a career and have accumulated mostly dormant assets, perhaps the best, safest, and simplest way to achieve guaranteed income is by exchanging some of your dormant assets for a pure income-only annuity purchased from an insurance company. We call this the *Covered Asset Strategy*.

Here is how it works:

The mutual insurance companies we work with provide other vehicles, including longevity insurance, the reciprocal to life insurance. The foundational purpose of life insurance is to protect against a premature death. The foundational purpose of longevity insurance is protection from outliving your money. It is also known as a pure income annuity.

This type of annuity is a contractual arrangement with an insurance company. You give the insurance company a specific dollar amount and they in return pay you an income for as long as you live. If you live for 50 years, they pay you for 50 years. If you live for 10 years, they only pay you for 10 years. The insurance company can make money from this product because of actuarial science. The company knows exactly how many of the pool of people who buy an annuity will pass away in any given year. They're making a bet, backed by actuarial science, not on your individual death, but on the expected death rate within the group of annuity holders. Some people are going to live for a long time, some people are going to live to an average life expectancy, and some people are going to die early.

The covered asset approach is designed so that if you enter into this type of arrangement, you have the equivalent dollar amount in life insurance. The life insurance protects your estate from the downside of an annuity: premature death. If you were to pass away prematurely, the annuity would stop, and the life insurance would pay out. The recommended ratio is 1:1. For every $1 annuitized, there is a $1 in life insurance coverage.

In the run-up years to retirement, your policy is established by allocating a portion of earned income to a 401(k) or IRA. As you make the transition to the retirement stage, the role of the insurance plan changes. Not only does it protect your family against the loss of the annuity income if you prematurely pass, but the cash value and dividend growth could become supplemental income, as well.

If we use Bryan's situation as an example and he decided to exchange all $1.5 million of his 401(k) with the insurance company for a guaranteed income for life, the Covered

Asset Strategy requires you to establish $1.5 million in life insurance.

Over the coming years, Bryan would have more than $1.5 million in permanent life insurance coverage, which wouldn't require any future premiums to maintain (if the policy was set up accordingly). One of the options when he decides to leave his employment is that he could exchange all $1.5 million in his 401(k) for a guaranteed income for life.

Another option Bryan would have as his policy builds is to convert it to an annuity using a Section 1035 tax-free exchange. There's no government restriction on when he can take money from an annuity. He can start whenever he wants.

Income annuities have many advantages. Rather than the Monte Carlo 3 to 4 percent annual payout rate for a 401(k) (with only a 90 percent chance you will *not* run out of money), income annuities can pay 6 percent or higher and guarantee the income for life.

The primary reason the percentage is so low is due to the sequence of return risk. What this means is that as the market fluctuates, the retiree is taking money out. When the market declines, the impact of that decline is magnified by the withdrawal, making it impossible for the portfolio to rebound.

The typical financial advisor will show you average rates of returns in the market and use that as the benchmark to give you advice on how much distribution to take.

Let's use the absolute best 30 years in the market, which were between 1970 and 1999. Over those years, the S&P average return was 10.85 percent.

If you had accumulated $1,000,000 in a portfolio and had it in the market, the predominant theory would assume you could take out easily $100,000 a year without running out of money and still be able to pass on $545,547 to your heirs.

Year	Beg. of Year Acct. Value	Earnings Rate	Annual Cash Flow	Interest Earnings	End of Year Acct. Value
1970	1,000,000	10.85%	(100,000)	97,650	997,650
1971	997,650	10.85%	(100,000)	97,395	995,045
1972	995,045	10.85%	(100,000)	97,112	992,157
1973	992,157	10.85%	(100,000)	96,799	988,956
1974	988,956	10.85%	(100,000)	96,452	985,408
1975	985,408	10.85%	(100,000)	96,067	981,475
1976	981,475	10.85%	(100,000)	95,640	977,115
1977	977,115	10.85%	(100,000)	95,167	972,282
1978	972,282	10.85%	(100,000)	94,643	966,925
1979	966,925	10.85%	(100,000)	94,061	960,986
1980	960,986	10.85%	(100,000)	93,417	954,403
1981	954,403	10.85%	(100,000)	92,703	947,106
1982	947,106	10.85%	(100,000)	91,911	939,017
1983	939,017	10.85%	(100,000)	91,033	930,050
1984	930,050	10.85%	(100,000)	90,060	920,110
1985	920,110	10.85%	(100,000)	88,982	909,092
1986	909,092	10.85%	(100,000)	87,787	896,879
1987	896,879	10.85%	(100,000)	86,461	883,340
1988	883,340	10.85%	(100,000)	84,992	868,333
1989	868,333	10.85%	(100,000)	83,364	851,697
1990	851,697	10.85%	(100,000)	81,559	833,256
1991	833,256	10.85%	(100,000)	79,558	812,814
1992	812,814	10.85%	(100,000)	77,340	790,155
1993	790,155	10.85%	(100,000)	74,882	765,036
1994	765,036	10.85%	(100,000)	72,156	737,193
1995	737,193	10.85%	(100,000)	69,135	706,328
1996	706,328	10.85%	(100,000)	65,787	672,115
1997	672,115	10.85%	(100,000)	62,074	634,189
1998	634,189	10.85%	(100,000)	57,960	592,149
1999	592,149	10.85%	(100,000)	53,398	545,547
Totals		10.85%	(3,000,000)	2,545,547	545,547

However, when you plug in market data, the story is a bit different. You end up running out of money in 1980—year 11.

Year	Beg. of Year Acct. Value	Earnings Rate	Annual Cash Flow	Interest Earnings	End of Year Acct. Value
1970	1,000,000	0.10%	(100,000)	880	900,880
1971	900,880	10.79%	(100,000)	86,389	887,269
1972	887,269	15.63%	(100,000)	123,076	910,345
1973	910,345	(17.37%)	(100,000)	(140,721)	669,624
1974	669,624	(29.72%)	(100,000)	(169,281)	400,343
1975	400,343	31.55%	(100,000)	94,755	395,098
1976	395,098	19.15%	(100,000)	56,507	351,605
1977	351,605	(11.50%)	(100,000)	(28,939)	222,665
1978	222,665	1.06%	(100,000)	1,303	123,968
1979	123,968	12.31%	(100,000)	2,950	26,918
1980	26,918	25.77%	(26,918)	0	0
1981	0	(9.73%)	0	0	0
1982	0	14.76%	0	0	0
1983	0	17.27%	0	0	0
1984	0	1.40%	0	0	0
1985	0	26.33%	0	0	0
1986	0	14.62%	0	0	0
1987	0	2.04%	0	0	0
1988	0	12.40%	0	0	0
1989	0	27.25%	0	0	0
1990	0	(6.56%)	0	0	0
1991	0	26.30%	0	0	0
1992	0	4.46%	0	0	0
1993	0	7.06%	0	0	0
1994	0	(1.54%)	0	0	0
1995	0	23.11%	0	0	0
1996	0	20.26%	0	0	0
1997	0	31.01%	0	0	0
1998	0	26.69%	0	0	0
1999	0	19.51%	0	0	0
Totals	0	10.85%	(1,026,000)	26,918	0

Because of market volatility, you can't bet on the average rate of return. Instead, you need to use a Monte Carlo simulation to determine safe withdrawal rates.

An income annuity will typically pay out at 6 percent or higher in our currently low interest rate environment. Annuity income isn't based on the stock market, so you're protected from market swings.

The tradeoff is when you set up a pure income annuity, your heirs don't get an inheritance, because there's nothing left over. There are provisions for survivor benefits, but they take away from the amount of income. That's why the ideal scenario is to secure coverage that will pay out to your estate.

STRATEGY #2: THE VOLATILITY BUFFER

The volatility buffer is another option that is typically used in conjunction with the Covered Asset Strategy. The idea is keep your money in your portfolio, such as your 401(k), or other volatile asset class that does not perform consistently year over year. You strategically withdraw the money depending on what the market is doing in that year.

Here's how it works:

Let's assume you are in the position to begin withdrawing money from your 401(k). Market inconsistency is what leads to using the Monte Carlo method so you don't withdraw too much. However, if you had a separate pool of capital that was interest-bearing and not correlated to the respective market, you could buffer the volatility by making withdrawals from it the year after a flat or market decline. That would allow your portfolio or other asset to rebound.

The cash value in your Wealth Maximization Account

acts as the ideal, non-correlated account and activates the volatility buffer strategy.

Let's use the same 1970 to 1999 period, now using the volatility buffer. You could take out $100,000 per year for over 23 years if you had a separate pool of money that was large enough to cover six years of volatility buffer.

Year	Beg. of Year Acct. Value	Earnings Rate	Annual Cash Flow	Interest Earnings	End of Year Acct. Value
1970	1,000,000	0.10%	(100,000)	880	900,880
1971	900,880	10.79%		97,176	998,056
1972	998,056	15.63%	(100,000)	140,395	1,038,451
1973	1,038,451	(17.37%)	(100,000)	(162,967)	775,484
1974	775,484	(29.72%)		(230,459)	545,025
1975	545,025	31.55%		171,950	716,975
1976	716,975	19.15%	(100,000)	118,141	735,116
1977	735,116	(11.50%)	(100,000)	(73,051)	562,065
1978	562,065	1.06%		5,969	568,035
1979	568,035	12.31%		69,918	637,953
1980	637,953	25.77%	(100,000)	138,650	676,603
1981	676,603	(9.73%)	(100,000)	(56,106)	520,497
1982	520,497	14.76%		76,832	597,329
1983	597,329	17.27%	(100,000)	85,894	583,223
1984	583,223	1.40%	(100,000)	6,768	489,991
1985	489,991	26.33%		129,031	619,023
1986	619,023	14.62%	(100,000)	75,859	594,882
1987	594,882	2.04%	(100,000)	10,075	504,957
1988	504,957	12.40%		62,596	567,552
1989	567,552	27.25%	(100,000)	127,410	594,963
1990	594,963	(6.56%)	(100,000)	(32,451)	462,511
1991	462,511	26.30%		121,654	584,165
1992	584,165	4.46%	(100,000)	21,614	505,780
1993	505,780	7.06%	(100,000)	28,628	434,408
1994	434,408	(1.54%)	(100,000)	(5,147)	329,260
1995	329,260	34.11%		112,313	441,573
1996	441,573	20.26%	(100,000)	69,215	410,789
1997	410,789	31.01%	(100,000)	96,370	407,158
1998	407,158	26.69%	(100,000)	81,965	389,124
1999	389,124	19.51%	(100,000)	56,409	345,533
Totals		10.85%	(2,000,000)	1,345,533	345,533

The volatility buffer concept also applies to investments like real estate or commodities. In fact, it applies to any investment that has any probability to not pay out the anticipated cash flow.

INTEGRATING THE PERPETUAL WEALTH STRATEGY

The Perpetual Wealth Strategy is the integration of insurance-based financial products with your financial life to enhance your overall objectives. The case has been made for its use in the building phase of wealth just as much as in the transition to the income phase.

This strategy comes with the necessity of commitment. The difference between insurance and traditional retirement savings vehicles like a Roth IRA, a 401(k), or a mutual fund, is that the latter are voluntary contributions. You don't have to contribute to them every year. When you set up a Wealth Maximization Account, you are contractually obligating yourself to certain contributions, known as premium payments, every year.

The commitment period is the first four and seven years of the plan, where a heightened level of discipline is needed. After that initial capitalization period, you have flexibility for your future contributions. When we help clients set up these policies, we typically structure them as a function of their earned income, other cash flow, and liquid cash. We set them up to align with your current financial situation so you can fulfill the commitment and pay every year without feeling financial stress. Although you can make modifications to the plan to reduce the obligation after the first year, you typically cannot go back to the original plan.

After you've met that initial commitment, the goal is to continue funding, which builds your wealth and your capacity to leverage the loan provision for the acquisition of more assets. After the initial funding period, it isn't uncommon for our clients to add to their strategy by opening plans on their children for college funding and other purposes, as well as new accounts on themselves. Remember, there is no government-dictated limit to how many Wealth Maximization Accounts you can own. To date, I own 17. My first policies were on me and my wife, Synthia, and were relatively small. We then opened accounts on our kids, then on my parents, and then bigger ones for us. The integration of The Perpetual Wealth Strategy can start small and then grow over time to keep up with your growth as your wealth increases.

KEY TAKEAWAYS

- To align with human nature, the end goal shouldn't be retirement but financial freedom.
- As you near retirement age, you're in a phase of your

life where you still have a lot to offer. Continually producing and creating value helps you maintain vitality and quality of life.

- The sooner you prepare for your post-retirement years, the better.
- You might be able to retire from your current circumstances early, if you can generate half of your current cash flow as earned income in your second career. That's easier than you may think in our modern era.
- Employment is evolving in the US. Tenured individuals have many new opportunities.
- The key to an abundant financial life is to maximize personal income and maximize the cash flow from your assets.
- Shifting your financial life to align with The Perpetual Wealth Strategy may not be easy. My experience, based on working with thousands of clients, has taught me that getting educated takes time, energy, focus, and commitment. However, your new approach will create an abundance of possibilities and completely change your life.
- Let's get started—I'll tell you how in the next chapter.

CHAPTER 13

MAKE THE SHIFT

SETTING UP YOUR WEALTH MAXIMIZATION ACCOUNT

If you do not change direction, you may end up where you are heading.

—LAO TZU

You don't need me if you want to buy what you've been learning about. You can find very reputable mutual insurance companies, but typically they don't sell insurance to you directly. You'll have to track down one of their representatives to make the purchase and trust that they're competent to set it up the right way.

TOP MAJOR MUTUAL INSURANCE COMPANIES

- New York Life
- MassMutual
- Penn Mutual
- Northwestern Mutual
- OneAmerica
- Lafayette Life
- Ohio National
- Guardian
- Ameritas
- Security Mutual of New York
- Mutual Trust Life

WORKING WITH A FINANCIAL PROFESSIONAL

A financial advisor or insurance agent may be licensed and contracted with a viable mutual company to do this for you, but very few are trained to give you truly objective advice. They're trained to sell you financial products like securities, IRAs, 529 plans, mutual funds, variable life insurance, or variable annuities.

Implementing The Perpetual Wealth Strategy contradicts their formal training on financial planning. I understand this contradiction firsthand. I've put in years of continuing education, certification courses and tests, licensing courses and tests, financial company trainings, and seminars. The financial philosophy I have been teaching you doesn't exist in these formal financial industry trainings. You can say the conventional financial planning industry has a monopoly on personalized advice.

It is vitally important for you to know up front that the financial advisors who subscribe to the principles and strategies that make up this book are extremely rare, but they're out there.

INTERVIEWING A FINANCIAL ADVISOR

How can you tell if a financial advisor has the skills to help you go beyond routine advice? Ask the right questions. If you don't already have a relationship with a financial or insurance advisor, here's what to ask when you interview them:

- What are the best strategies to grow wealth? (This will help you determine their financial philosophy.)
- What is the role of dividend-paying whole life in a financial strategy?
- How do you personally use whole life as part of a personalized financial strategy?
- Do you include a Paid-Up Additions rider to the policies?
- How do you structure the Paid-Up Additions rider when you set up a policy?

- How do you use the MEC limit or 7-pay limit to structure a policy?
- What mutual companies do you work with?
- What's your personal financial strategy? (You want to ensure they practice what they preach.)
- Tell me how you have used your insurance to build your family's wealth.
- Would you explain some examples, as well as those of your clients?

Ask for client references, testimonials, and case studies from clients like you.

You want to feel certain of their competency to add value to your life and advise you based on your objectives and best interests.

A typical financial advisor isn't going to offer you life insurance, especially a policy structured according to the characteristics of a Wealth Maximization Account. You'll need to ask for it specifically and perhaps teach them about it.

WEALTH MAXIMIZATION ACCOUNT CRITERIA

- Underwritten by a highly rated mutual insurance company
- Dividend-paying whole life
- Paid-Up Additions rider
- Funded at 7-pay or MEC level
- Guaranteed loan against cash value

Your advisor might not know very much about these criteria. If you're committed to staying with your local or family advisor, you could ask them to learn about it, get the proper licenses and contracts with a mutual company, and try to figure it out.

A better approach might be sticking with your existing financial advisor for your other financial accounts and looking for someone who already understands what you need for wealth maximization.

It might be easier to work with somebody who is already an expert—a Wealth Strategist like those who work with me at Paradigm Life.

We're the experts.

We work with your current financial team, such as your financial advisor, accountant, or attorney. Additionally, we are trained to be your comprehensive financial guide—

what we call a Wealth Strategist. We can help you set up a WMA the right way. If you don't have them already, we can introduce you to our network of legal professionals, accounting professionals, attorneys, investment providers, and more, all based on your situation.

KEY TAKEAWAYS

- Take care and take control when selecting the financial advisor you want assisting you in setting up a WMA. There are questions that you can ask that will help you determine whether they know what they are talking about.
- Know what you want going into an appointment with a financial advisor.
- Make sure to choose a financial advisor who subscribes to the principles and strategies you want to implement.

CHAPTER 14

═══════════

TAKE BACK CONTROL

There is something fundamentally unfair about a government that takes away so much of people's money, power, and personal control while telling them that life will be better as a result.

—STEVE FORBES

We live in unprecedented times, a world that would never have been predicted even 50 years ago. Of course, uncertainty, conflict, and chaos are part of the experience, but if you think about it, it has always been that way.

Regardless of the anxiety, our human nature compels us to grow, discover, and capitalize on the limited time we have here. Ultimately, when it comes to my paradigm of money, uncertainty and control are mutually exclusive. The more control you have, the less risk you have, and a

:r hope for a positive outcome. The more educated :e, the more control you have.

Embrace not just a new mindset, but reality. Embrace your current situation and what your future is based on. Embrace your potential and the opportunity to create an amazing life for yourself and your family.

You may have an idea of what your ideal future is, your ideal career, full or partial retirement, or the ideal place to live.

Part of taking massive action toward these outcomes is taking back control of your life, which includes your finances. The first step is identifying where you are. What are you doing, and why are you doing it? What are the biggest obstacles in the way of achieving your ideal life?

Will you be able to claim absolute control right away and be bulletproof from forces in the outside world? No.

Changes in the economy and society will affect you. That's the environment we play in, where we don't always know what's going to happen. The more control you have, the more agile you're going to be during shifts in the economic and business cycles.

Human nature is evolution in progress. As we get smarter,

things are going to change and affect our course. In 1990, very few people understood the nature of the internet. In 2007, nobody knew what Facebook was or had a smartphone. Things will happen in the future that we can't imagine right now, but they will become an instrumental part of our lives, especially if we allow flexibility in our financial strategy.

Ideas of the past may have worked once, but not anymore. You need to be agile to respond to future changes.

Identify yourself as your number-one asset, and make sure that you're always getting educated, always figuring out ways to be of value to other people, because that is the true way to build and maintain lasting wealth.

Use the abundance of intellectual and physical resources available to you to create financial freedom for yourself.

> *"It's not the lack of resources, it's your lack of resourcefulness that stops you."*
>
> —TONY ROBBINS

The primary difference between iconic businessmen and women is their degree of resourcefulness. Are you taking control of your destiny and optimizing the resources around you, or are you putting it in the hands of someone else?

If your work is causing you pain, stress, and anxiety, quit. If you're miserable in your work environment and stay simply to have a paycheck and put money away for the future, then you need to cut that at the root as soon as possible. Leave now. It's not worth it.

If you don't like your job, take your skills, reinvent yourself, and find something that is fulfilling. Exchange your skills for doing that, and you're going to get paid.

This sounds very utopian, like one of those perfect-world scenarios. But, it's more realistic today than ever.

Manage risk. What I've been talking about in this entire book is a way for you to identify, manage, and mitigate your financial risks—and actually gain at the same time. Most people think that if they take less risk, they are going to earn less money. It doesn't have to be that way. In fact, history has shown that taking on more risk to earn higher returns has often produced the opposite result.

Identify any personal risks, aversions, or anxieties you may have regarding your finances. Manage these through discipline and implementation of proper education. Then, mitigate them with The Wealth Maximization Account as your financial bedrock.

Taking advantage of the information in this book puts you

one step closer to taking control. The question is, will you take advantage of the expertise that my team has to offer?

WHERE MY TEAM FITS IN

I run two companies—Paradigm Life, an independent insurance agency; and PL Wealth Advisors, a Registered Investment Advisory firm. We have clients in every state in the US and every province in Canada. We conduct our business using modern communication technology, such as video conferences and webinars. We provide all our training and educational resources online, for free. Our website at paradigmlife.net has thousands of hours of online video and courses, so anyone can learn about what we do.

What we do is simple. We're committed to financial education—empowering people to take back control of their financial destiny instead of handing it to Wall Street. We do this by educating people about the financial products we offer, our financial strategies, and our financial philosophy. We educate business owners and investors to maximize their growth while mitigating avoidable risks. We consult with families as to the best way to provide for their kids' financial future. We teach those who have accumulated wealth and have been preparing for retirement, to accelerate that time frame and achieve financial freedom much sooner.

We implement a personalized financial strategy—The Perpetual Wealth Strategy—for each client.

Our methods aren't new. They are based on the traditional approach to financial planning that was used before 401(k) s, mutual funds, and the Wall Street/banking monopoly became standard. We use the specific integration of insurance-based financial products that have been around for well over 150 years. They've been proven to work repeatedly. They outperform typical financial planning and mitigate your risk of loss substantially.

The strategy integrates insurance-based financial products into each of the three primary financial stages of life that everyone is in at one point or another: growth, income, legacy.

The philosophy of The Perpetual Wealth Strategy is not to focus on the mirage that awaits you at the end of a 30- or 40-year career—what we commonly refer to as retirement. It is to achieve financial freedom as soon as possible. Discover your calling and turn it into a career. Find a meaningful way to take the best of you and offer it to others in the form of a service or product.

OUR SERVICES

At Paradigm Life, we focus on education first. Learning

how to utilize our unique financial tools is important to us because we know that it can change your life. We start with our online courses and digital assets, which are mostly free. We teach you about the financial products we sell and how they benefit you. We teach you another perspective of the stock market, how investment real estate works, unique business and tax strategies, entrepreneurship, and more.

We provide financial guidance related to how The Wealth Maximization Account helps in your unique situation. We also provide the services to set up your first or next WMA.

Whether you're just starting out, are getting ready for retirement, or are somewhere in-between. Our services can help you.

We work with business owners who do well in their business and want more flexibility and control with their personal financial strategy.

PICK THE RIGHT FINANCIAL TEAM

If you resonate with what I've been saying, this is what we live and breathe every day. We specialize in helping our clients improve their financial situations. That's what we do—nothing else. We're experts.

represent all the top mutual life insurance companies.

But you need more than just insurance advice. You need business, legal, tax, and investment advice. You need mortgage, property, and casualty insurance. You need estate and business planning. You might even need life coaching to find out what your purpose is. We're partnered with an extensive network of skilled professionals who share our philosophy. We can connect you to the right people for your needs and your overall financial health.

We've worked with thousands of clients and have thousands of case studies. We're always learning and tweaking, so we're always improving. You benefit from all that experience.

WHAT'S THE NEXT STEP?

You can learn more about me and my team at headsortail-siwin.com or at paradigmlife.net. That's where you can access all our materials, including our videos, podcasts, online courses, and more.

You can set up a no-obligation, no-cost consultation to see how our products and strategies apply to your situation just by clicking the "Schedule an appointment" link. We'll set you up with the right Wealth Strategist at a time of your choosing.

Our Wealth Strategists have been chosen for their high caliber and dedication to our clients' well-being. They embody the Paradigm values, strategies, and philosophy. They're paid only through predetermined, fixed compensation from the insurance companies. We typically don't charge front-end fees.

RESOURCES

When Paradigm Life started in 2007, people still wanted to do business face-to-face. They weren't comfortable doing business with someone they'd never met before. They wanted to do more due diligence and learn more about us. In response, we started to put everything we do online. Our website at paradigmlife.net has courses, webinars, recommended reading, e-books, and a lot more. We have a YouTube channel with a ton of informative videos. We've done well over 200 episodes of our podcast *The Wealth Standard* (thewealthstandard.com).

Having all our information online is our way of letting clients get to know us before they do business with us.

PARTNER WITH ME

Working with Paradigm Life and PL Wealth Advisors can be a rewarding career for a financial professional. It's challenging and requires a great deal of effort, training, technological proficiency, and willingness to let go of the typical financial planning philosophy.

If you're a financial advisor, financial planner, or insurance agent with at least three years of experience in the financial services industry, you can partner with Paradigm Life and PL Wealth Advisors in ways that could be very rewarding.

The future of the typical financial advisor is uncertain, as is the entire financial services industry. If you are ready for a fulfilling and meaningful career, we would love to talk. Visit us at www.headsortailsiwin.com/advisor.

CONTACT ME

I wrote this book to help people discover a better way to manage their finances and the means to achieve financial freedom. The information I've presented here is complex and I'm sure you still have questions. My team and I would like to answer them personally. Please call us at 855-238-1833, email me at headsiwin@paradigmlife.net, connect with me on LinkedIn, Instagram, or Facebook, or message me through Paradigm Life's Facebook page, www.facebook.com/paradigmlife.

EPILOGUE

For me, 2017 was a pivotal year for me and for Paradigm Life.

It began with a small goal-setting session called "The Perfect Life Workshop," hosted by my good friend Craig Ballantyne. Only four business owners/entrepreneurs attended the 10-hour session. We worked through some deep questions and scenarios about our lives and businesses, such as, "Twenty years from now, what would you regret not doing or achieving?"

The discussion and sharing brought to the surface realizations and emotions that forced me to dig even deeper and ask myself some difficult questions, such as: What are you doing? And, what are you *really* doing? What matters most to you and do your activities confirm or conflict with these priorities? What's missing from your life?

My business and life were coasting along at this juncture. We had a lot of clients and great recurring revenue; my investments were doing well. The family was in good shape. However, I began to realize that I was shouldering a lot of anxiety, pressure, and lack of fulfillment that I just wasn't addressing, and the burden had been growing. It was all coming to a head.

The significance of this retreat came on the heels of news that knocked my entire immediate family out of rhythm and made those questions even more profound.

Two days earlier, my brother, Tom, called me just as we arrived home from a 10-hour drive from Denver, where our families had spent the holidays with my parents. Tom informed us that he was at the hospital with his 12-year-old daughter, Myleigh. The doctors were telling him she might have cancer. Just a few hours later, the diagnosis was confirmed. It was my job to inform our parents who were arriving that evening by train. I can still hear my mom's emotional breakdown when I told her the news.

After the workshop, which happened to be in Denver, I headed over to the Children's Hospital. I spent about 20 minutes in the waiting room gaining composure, then went into Myleigh's room just as the doctors were presenting the official results. It was stage three non-Hodgkin's lymphoma. The treatment plan would be several months of chemotherapy, followed by radiation treatment.

Our families are close, and Tom is one of my best friends. We all felt the blow.

This series of events caused me to re-evaluate everything in my life. I had to confront the friction I was dealing with and make a course correction, starting with my team at Paradigm Life.

THE PARADIGM CULTURE

I began by writing a three-year vision statement, guided by the book *Double Double* by Cameron Herold. He emphasizes the vital importance of showing your team the path you are on and where you're going. The process of creating that statement was paramount to gaining clarity about what I saw as the future of the business.

I spent a few months identifying and defining my personal values, then clarified our company's values to ensure that they promoted a culture that would thrive. The results were as expected. The behavior and attitude of some individuals in the company didn't align with our values. Over the next few months, many of them resigned or were let go.

The course correction provided the environment for the

team to come together. It helped us bring on new team members who were naturally aligned with our mission and values.

I consider my team part of my family. Preserving and prospering our culture is my top business initiative—my mission. I love coming to the office and witnessing the passion and drive of our team. One of my core beliefs is that a healthy and thriving work culture is vital to individual well-being. It's also essential for a meaningful client experience. Our mission is to provide the very best education, customer support, and solutions to help our valued clients achieve their dreams.

THE PROSPERITY ECONOMICS MOVEMENT

During this transitional period, I sought refuge and counsel from my dear friends Kim Butler and Todd Langford. They've been my colleagues and mentors for many years. I headed down for a few days to their little slice of heaven in a small Texas town called Mt. Enterprise. Their insight and feedback were invaluable and helped me solidify the path I was on regarding Paradigm.

The visit also opened the door to joining the leadership of a 501(c)(3) nonprofit called the Prosperity Economics Movement (PEM). Kim started the movement in 2014 and now spends half of her busy life planning events, creating materials, and writing books to educate financial advisors and individuals about our principles, strategies, and philosophy. It is a labor of love and demands a great deal of time and effort, but it is changing lives by opening a doorway for the financial services industry.

At PEM, we are building a network of financial advisors who are questioning the typical financial planning model—realizing that it is flawed and no longer suitable for the well-being of most clients. Alternatives exist, and PEM is a guide for them to transform the broker-dealer, securities-based financial practice world.

PEM has fostered a network of professionals, including investment providers, estate and legacy-planning attorneys, business attorneys, accountants, bookkeepers, mortgage and reverse mortgage lenders, and others. The network is continuously growing.

If you are a financial advisor or business professional and would like to learn more about the movement and how you can get involved, please visit us at prosperityeconomicsadvisors.com.

If you are a client and want to learn more about the movement, visit prosperitypeaks.com, a website dedicated to teaching you about your financial options.

Those monumental events set a course for enhanced growth and greater possibilities, including this book.

If you have read this far, I want to sincerely thank you. Writing a book is more difficult than I imagined. It means more than you know to realize that you have absorbed more than a decade's worth of experience, insight, and learning.

Thank you for reading, and best wishes on your path to financial freedom.

ACKNOWLEDGMENTS

I have so many people to thank, it's overwhelming. I have been influenced by some of the greatest minds in business—very little of what I do and who I am is original. I sincerely thank all of you who I have had the privilege of working with over the years. You have shaped me into a better father, husband, advisor, leader, and human being.

I specifically want to acknowledge the team at Scribe Media and Lioncrest Publishing for their patience, persistence, and flexibility working with my chaotic schedule. Thank you to those who read through drafts and provided incredible insight and perspective, especially Nick Welch and David Hymas.

To Kim and Todd, my mentors and friends over the years, thank you for your dedication to our principles despite adversity, and for your commitment to teaching advisors the truth about money, investing, and financial advice.

To Nelson Nash, thank you for your wisdom, relentless drive, and willingness to share. Thanks to David, Carlos, and Bob at NNI for carrying his mission forward.

To my brothers Tom and John, and my parents John and Patty, thanks for your love, support, and prayers throughout the years.

Thanks to my mentors, coaches, advisors, partners, and friends for your teaching, support, and sharing your gifts with me over the years. In no specific order, I thank Garrett Gunderson, Les McGuire, Greg Blackbourn, Jason Hartman, Garrett White, Ben and Marv Curtis, Dan Torsak, Matt Smith, Jeff Schneider, Tom Wheelwright, Ken McElroy, Josh and Lisa Lannon, Andy Tanner, Mark Ford, Blair Singer, Tom Dyson, Tim Mittelstaedt, Mike Dillard, Robert Hirsch, Brian and Jake Fouts, Naresh Vissa, Dale Richards, Craig Ballantyne, Rebecca Rice, Robert Helms, Russell Gray, Ray Poteet, Barry Dyke, Mike Isom, Connor Boyack, Pat Foley, Scott Davison, Doug Gritton, Jason Rink, and Thom Finn.

To all those Paradigm Life team members along the way who graced the office and contributed to who and what we are today, in alphabetical order: Christian Allen, Craig

Allen, David Allen, Tanya Alofipo, Preston Alvey, Rick Andra, Danaka Andrews, Sara Arrowood, Don Ashby, Erica Ashby, Lauren Ashley, Justin Atkinson, Chris Badger, Heather Balchinclowing, Spring Bastow, Pete Bennett, Mike Berg, Michael Bonny, Wade Borth, Barry Brooksby, Dwayne Burnell, Nick Burton, Kim Butler, Nate Butler, Rebecca Calandro, Jacob Calata, Kayeliann Calveri, John Cattan, Beth Chandler, Chase Chandler, Ryan Clark, Sam Close, Rich Clouse, Kathy Cole, Jacqueline Collins, Spencer Couch, Tim Croteau, Ben Curtis, Marv Curtis, Matthew Dean, Sam Denton, Ben Dickson, John Donohoe, Synthia Donohoe, Nick Drzayich, Kent Dunn, Brent Elswick, Bill Fagergren, Anthony Faso, Sheri Fawson, Solana Fawson, Bri Fitzgerald, Sean Fleming, Ashley Forsberg, Levi Forsberg, Braden Galloway, Brian Gee, Nick Geister, Brad Gibb, Sarbloh Gill, Kelly Gilbert, Jason, Gillham, Brent Gritton, Brian Gutierrez, Jennifer Hamilton, Chester Hansen, Chad Hanson, Keith Hargrove, Joseph Harris, Travis Hays, Victoria Heaps, Mark Hemingway, Tim Hemingway, Shireen Hosseini, David Hymas, Amanda Inukihaangana, Michael Isom, Jim Jackson, Deborah Jacobs, Jeff Jaramillo, Nick Jensen, Ashley Johnson, K'sun Joseph, Trever Keele, Noah Kelsch, Catherine Kiene, Jim Kindred, Steve Kitchen, Jared Lainhart, Tim Lawler, Bonnie Layne, Ryan Lee, Nick Litster, Ben Lonsdale, Norma Lopez, Chelcie Loutensock, Jayson Lowe, Abby Lunt, Milena Margaryan, Justin Martin, Curtis May, Tracey May, Bryan McCloskey, Kennan McDonough,

Jonathan McFall, Eric McGuire, Kody McKinley, Kathy McNamara, Bryn McWhorter, Gabe Meola, George Moleli, Lib Montoya, Russ Morgan, Sabrina Mourigan, Joey Mure, Braun Myers, Leo Naranjo, Brandon Neibel, Justin Nelson, Michelle Olsen, Jake Orton, Cody Ostler, Jim Ostler, Kylie Painter, McKenzie Painter, Millie Parkinson, Eric Patterson, Travis Peay, Duncan Peterson, Heidi Pincock, Gary Pinkerton, Bryan Repple, Becky Rice, Boby Richards, Kayla Richards, Dallin Rogers, Eric Roy, Alicia Sanchez, Anna Schovaers, Chad Sellers, KJ Shurtleff, Ross Simon, Bill Skinner, Todd Skinner, Lauren Slaughter, Brett "Chunga" Smith, Chandler Smith, David Smith, Micah Stainbrook, Carli Stauffer, Jennie Steed, Jessica Stevens, Whitney Stevens, John Stewart, Will Street, Todd Strobel, Kraig Strom, Verena Takai, Martell Taylor, Michelle Taylor, Paula Taylor, Randy Taylor, Janae Telford, Allie Thompson, Jake Thompson, Catherine Timpson, Cinta Tofete, Sulu Tofete, Alex Topolewski, Dan Torsak, David Torsak, Kylie Twomey, Spencer Ure, Matt Valentine, Burgandy Van Wagenen, Josh Varney, Matt Walters, Danielle Wardle, Brennan Waters, Camden Weight, Nick Welch, Garrett White, Derek Williams, Leslie Williams, Cristina Wilson, Jennifer Winder, Sam Wright, Taylor Wright, Joshua Youngbluth, Rod Zabriskie, Martin Zepeda, Lorin Zitting, Jaden Zubal.

ABOUT THE AUTHOR

PATRICK DONOHOE is the founder and CEO of Paradigm Life and PL Wealth Advisors—companies founded to educate clients to reach financial freedom by building wealth, creating cash flow, and establishing a legacy. Since 2007, they have helped thousands of individuals in all 50 states and every province in Canada efficiently grow their wealth by using financial strategies outside of the typical Wall Street solutions.

Patrick is a popular speaker at wealth management, investment, and personal development seminars and hosts *The Wealth Standard* podcast, a highly regarded financial podcast.

Patrick grew up in West Hartford, Connecticut and moved to Salt Lake City in 2003 to attend the University of Utah, where he received his BA degree in economics. He lives in Salt Lake City with his wife and three children. He enjoys hanging out with the family, vacationing, the summer, and sports—especially ice hockey.